Good Housekeeping

400
CALORIE

COMFORT
FOOD

Good Housekeeping

400 CALORIE

COMFORT FOOD

Easy Mix-and-Match Recipes for a Skinnier You!

HEARST BOOKS
New York

HEARST BOOKS
New York

An Imprint of Sterling Publishing
387 Park Avenue South
New York, NY 10016

GOOD HOUSEKEEPING
Rosemary Ellis
EDITOR IN CHIEF

Courtney Murphy
CREATIVE DIRECTOR

Susan Westmoreland
FOOD DIRECTOR

Samantha B. Cassetty, MS, RD
NUTRITION DIRECTOR

Sharon Franke
**KITCHEN APPLIANCES &
FOOD TECHNOLOGY DIRECTOR**

Book design: Memo Productions
Cover design: Jon Chaiet
Project editor: Sarah Scheffel
Photography credits on page 158

The Good Housekeeping Cookbook Seal guar-
antees that the recipes in this cookbook meet
the strict standards of the Good Housekeeping
Research Institute. The Institute has been a source
of reliable information and a consumer advocate
since 1900, and established its seal of approval in
1909. Every recipe has been triple-tested for ease,
reliability, and great taste.

www.goodhousekeeping.com

For information about custom editions, special
sales, and premium and corporate purchases,
please contact Sterling Special Sales at 800-805-
5489 or specialsales@sterlingpublishing.com.

Distributed in Canada by
Sterling Publishing
c/o Canadian Manda Group, 165 Dufferin Street
Toronto, Ontario, Canada M6K 3H6

Distributed in Australia by
Capricorn Link
(Australia) Pty. Ltd.
P.O. Box 704, Windsor, NSW 2756, Australia

Manufactured in China

2 4 6 8 10 9 7 5 3 1

Sterling ISBN: 978-1-61837-056-3

CONTENTS

315
CALORIES
Chicken Noodle Soup
(page 26)

FOREWORD

These days we're working longer and harder than ever, so a delicious, yet easy, dinner seems a just reward. This collection of recipes will help you plan those dinners and more without breaking the calorie bank. Whether you want to satisfy a pasta craving, make a hearty dish for a family get-together, or need help re-creating a childhood favorite, *400 Calorie Comfort Food* has answers for you. Warm-your-heart favorites that recall the dishes Mom (or maybe Grandma) used to make—old-fashioned mac and cheese, succulent beef stew, a side of mashed potatoes, and oatmeal cookies are all here—trimmed a bit to be delicious, not overindulgent.

With *400 Calorie Comfort Food*, we've made it easy to prepare these comforting favorites without a surplus of calories and fat. You'll love the ease of our slow-cooked stews, from Shrimp and Sausage Gumbo to classic Chicken Noodle Soup. Or, if speed is what's required, try our Smothered Pork Chops, Chicken-Fried Steak, or one of our other fast weeknight favorites. For special occasions, we've included a chapter on roasts like Honey-Mustard Chicken and Glazed Meat Loaf. And, of course, we haven't forgotten brunch specialties like Crustless Leek and Gruyère Quiche and Overnight Savory French Toast. Each recipe is 400 calories or less and includes complete nutritional information. Icons indicate heart-healthy, and high-fiber recipes, as well as thirty minute or less, make-ahead, and slow-cooker dishes.

To make meal-planning simple, the second half of the book includes recipes for satisfying sides, salads, and desserts. Irresistible add-ons like Sweet Potatoes with Marshmallow Meringue and Creamed Spinach round out comforting meals, while treats like Brownie Bites and Angel Food Cake deliver a sweet finale when you need one. For tips on meal planning, see "Skinny Comfort Food" on page 9. In "Smart Choices" and "The Right Ingredients" on pages 10 to 12, we provide advice on healthy, low-cal ingredients to ensure that your meals are not only low in calories but scrumptious, too!

SUSAN WESTMORELAND
Food Director, *Good Housekeeping*

INTRODUCTION

We all love comfort food favorites—old-fashioned mac and cheese, succulent roast chicken, a side of mashed potatoes, and creamy chocolate pudding. One bite of these soothing classics and the world instantly feels like a cozier, gentler place. But alongside the pleasure, we frequently experience guilt—just how many calories did that scrumptious meal cost us?

At *Good Housekeeping*, serving up family-pleasing comfort food has always been part of our mission. With *400 Calorie Comfort Food*, you can dig into sure-to-satisfy classics with no regrets. Here, we share 55 delicious 400-calorie (or less!) recipes for all your comfort food faves. You'll love our skinny takes on satisfyingly familiar dishes like French onion soup, pulled pork sandwiches, chicken-fried steak, shepherd's pie, and meat loaf. And, of course, we haven't forgotten to include low-cal versions of meatballs, French toast, potpie, or chili, either!

As the title of the book promises, every single main dish is 400 calories or less per serving, and as a bonus, we've included chapters on sides (and even skinny desserts!) that will help you round out your meals. From potatoes, stuffings, and breads to veggie dishes like Creamed Spinach and Broccoli Gratin to old-fashioned desserts such as Strawberry-Rhubarb Crisp and Angel Food Cake, the 35 add-on recipes are organized by calorie count—from lowest to highest. Simply choose your main dish, then use your surplus calories to select an add-on (or two!) that will make it a comforting meal.

For example, if you're watching your weight and limiting dinners to 500 calories, enjoy our Turkey Breast with Vegetable Gravy (285 calories) with a side of Broccoli Gratin (95 calories) and finish with one of our rich Cocoa Brownies (120 calories). 285 + 95 + 120 = 500 calories. With *Good Housekeeping 400 Calorie Comfort Food*, it's easy to prepare luscious low-calorie meals. See "Skinny Comfort Food," opposite, for tips on how to do it.

To help make meal planning even easier, we offer guidelines for preparing healthier comfort food (see "Smart Choices" on page 10), along with an overview of easy substitutions and healthy additions on pages 12 and 13. And, because the slow cooker is a convenient way to make comforting stews and roasts, we provide suggestions to help you get the most of this appliance on page 14.

SKINNY COMFORT FOOD

It may sound like an oxymoron, but planning satisfying, low-calorie breakfasts, lunches, and dinners is easy with *Good Housekeeping 400 Calorie Comfort Food*. Prepare the add-ons we've suggested with each main-dish recipe under "Make It a Meal" to create 500-calorie dinners, 400-calorie lunches and brunches, or 300-calorie breakfasts. Or get creative and choose from the sides and dessert recipe lists on pages 111, 125, and 137 to make your own satisfying meal combos. Here are some examples of yummy (and astoundingly skinny!) comfort food meals to get you started.

SAMPLE BRUNCH MENU

MAIN: Crustless Leek and Gruyère Quiche	260 calories
ADD-ON: Oven Fries	130 calories
Total calories per meal	**390 calories**

SAMPLE LUNCH MENU

MAIN: Chicken Noodle Soup	315 calories
ADD-ON: Chocolate Chip–Oatmeal Cookie	80 calories
Total calories per meal	**395 calories**

SAMPLE DINNER MENU

MAIN: Roasted Lemon Chicken	360 calories
ADD-ON 1: Vegetable-Herb Stuffing	90 calories
ADD-ON 2: Lemony Bean Duo	55 calories
Total calories per meal	**505 calories**

SMART CHOICES

It's no secret: Dishes like meat loaf, mac and cheese, and mashed potatoes taste oh-so-good, but they can wreak havoc on your waistline—not to mention your health. The good news: You can enjoy comfort food dishes like these if you keep the following guidelines in mind.

• **Focus on flavor.** While controlling calories and fat is a primary concern, providing mealtime satisfaction is also essential to achieving and maintaining a healthy weight. The truth is, if the food you make doesn't taste good, you and your family won't eat it. Happily, sticks of butter, dollops of sour cream, and heaps of bacon are not the only way to inject your meals with flavor.

Consider the flavor-enhancing possibilities of items like chicken and vegetable broths, pan juices, fresh herbs, zesty spices, and low- or nonfat condiments such as soy sauce, mustard, and hoisin sauce. We top our turkey breast with a luscious gravy that's made with roasted vegetables. Our Glazed Meat Loaf is bulked up with quick-cooking oats and glazed with a simple soy sauce–flavored ketchup. In the recipes throughout this book, you'll discover lots of other low-cal, high-flavor tricks that you can incorporate into your cooking.

• **Keep an eye on fat.** Consume less than 10 percent of total calories from saturated fats, per USDA guidelines. Saturated fats are concentrated in fatty animal-based foods; when an excess is consumed, it raises both your blood cholesterol level and your total calorie intake. Coat your pans with olive or canola oil; we recommend just a spritz of nonstick cooking spray for many of the dishes in this book. Whenever possible, we swap in reduced-fat dairy products and use egg whites instead of whole eggs; see "The Right Ingredients" on page 12 for more tips on substitutions. And, of course, limit animal-based fats like butter, red meat, and chicken skin. We do this by using trans-fat-free margarine in place of butter, bulking up ground beef with beans (or swapping in ground turkey or chicken), and removing chicken skin after cooking, so you get all of the flavor while limiting your fat intake.

• **Indulge—a little.** Sticking to a low-calorie diet is difficult if you don't allow yourself some judicious treats. In fact, we've selected all of the recipes in this book with that balance in mind. Our casseroles include a little cheese, our soups include some milk for creaminess, and we've included an entire chapter on skinny desserts.

390 CALORIES
*Chicken-Fried Steak
(page 41)*

THE RIGHT INGREDIENTS

Lighten up with these easy substitutions and healthy additions.

Swap in reduced-fat or low-fat dairy products. Choose reduced-fat cheese or low or reduced-fat milk, which inject creaminess and flavor into soups, casseroles, baked goods, and more. Our gooey French Onion Soup is made with reduced-fat Swiss cheese, for example, while our Lasagna Rolls use part-skim ricotta and mozzarella cheeses. Our Broccoli Mac and Cheese swaps in low-fat (1%) milk for whole, while our amazingly creamy Chocolate Pudding employs nonfat milk.

Use egg whites in addition to the whole egg. They contain almost zero fat and add lightness to dishes like our Ham and Cheese Soufflé and even our Chocolate Chip–Oatmeal Cookies. In some cases, egg whites do the job even better than yolks: The whites are top notch when it comes to making bread crumbs stick in our Oven-Fried Chicken Tenders.

Go for whole grain. To up your fiber quotient, swap in whole-wheat pasta, flour, and bread whenever possible. We've used whole-wheat breadcrumbs to top our Broccoli Mac and Cheese, whole-wheat flour to coat our Chicken-Fried Steak, and you can swap in whole-wheat products in our other recipes, too. If you want to swap in whole-wheat flour, for best results, use 50 percent whole-wheat flour and 50 percent white. Polenta, an Italian favorite made from coarsely ground cornmeal, is another great way to get your grains. Enjoy it in our Sausage and Polenta and in Polenta and Chili Potpie—these hearty, satisfying dishes may just become family favorites.

Eat your beans. They're packed with protein plus insoluble and soluble fiber, which have the wonderful benefit of making you feel fuller faster. Insoluble fiber also helps promote regularity,

CHOOSE CALORIE-CONSCIOUS CUTS

If you love your meat, swap in these lean cuts and shave off the calories—and fat—big time. (Calories are for 6 ounces of cooked meat, off the bone and sauce-free).

Pork: Instead of pork ribs (558 calories), try pork tenderloin (250 calories). You'll save an impressive 308 calories per serving and slash the fat, too.

Ground beef: Instead of 70% lean ground beef (464 calories), enjoy 95% lean ground beef (291 calories). You'll save 173 calories per serving. Or substitute ground turkey or ground chicken for a smart, low-fat alternative. Total calorie savings per serving is 292 for ground turkey and 251 for ground chicken.

Chicken: Instead of a chicken leg with skin (394 calories), cook a chicken breast without skin (280 calories). You'll save 114 calories per serving and reduce the fat, too.

and soluble fiber can reduce levels of LDL ("bad") cholesterol. Try intermixing beans with meat, as we've done in our Chipotle Beef Chili.

Add in fresh veggies. Comfort food is not all about cheese, potatoes, and bacon. Whether you incorporate vegetables into your main dish, as we've cleverly done in our Shrimp and Sausage Gumbo and beef-stuffed peppers, or enjoy a side of Apple Cider Greens or Sesame Ginger Sprouts, it's important to include vegetables—ideally all the colors of the rainbow!—in your meals for essential vitamins, fiber, antioxidants, and more. The cheese and bacon should be flavor enhancements, not the main event.

THE SKINNY ON SLOW COOKING

The slow cooker was made for comfort food! It allows you to prepare flavorful soups and stews and meltingly tender meat with a minimum of effort. Here are tips to ensure that you get the most out of your slow cooker.

• Prep the night before, and all you'll need to do in the morning is toss your ingredients into the slow-cooker bowl and flip the switch. (Measure ingredients, cut veggies, and trim fat from meats, then refrigerate components separately in bowls or storage bags.)

• Less tender cuts of meat and poultry—such as pork shoulder, chuck roast, beef brisket, and poultry legs—are best suited for slow cooking. Skim fat from cooking liquid when done. (Fish and other seafood aren't good options unless they're added in the last hour of cooking.)

• For richer flavor in stews, sprinkle meat and poultry with flour and brown it in a skillet before putting it in the slow cooker. (Be sure to scrape up the flavorful browned bits that stick to the bottom of the skillet and add them to the pot; they'll help thicken the sauce and enhance the flavor even more.)

• Resist the urge to take the lid off the cooker and stir the ingredients, especially in the early stages of warming—the pot will lose valuable heat.

• When you're cooking root vegetables, put them at the bottom of the pot—they cook more slowly than meat.

• Slow cooking tends to intensify flavorful spices and seasonings such as chili powder and garlic, so use them conservatively.

• Dried herbs may lessen in flavor, so adjust seasonings by stirring a little more in at the end of cooking. When using fresh herbs, save some to toss in at the last minute for fresh flavor and color.

FREEZE (AND REHEAT) WITH EASE

Many of the stews and casseroles in this book are perfect candidates for freezing. Make two and freeze one for double-duty dinners you can enjoy on a busy weeknight.

To freeze: Before freezing, refrigerate soups or stews for 30 minutes; casseroles need 30 minutes at room temperature plus 30 minutes in the fridge. Wrap casseroles tightly in foil or plastic wrap. Seal soups and stews in zip-tight plastic bags or freezer containers. To maximize space, stack bags horizontally until frozen, then store upright. Or line your baking dish with heavy-duty greased foil before making the casserole; once the meal is frozen solid, remove the frozen food and transfer it to a large zip-tight plastic bag.

To thaw soups and stews: Place frozen food, still sealed in a plastic bag, in a bowl or sink of hot water for 5 to 10 minutes or until it can be broken into pieces. If the food is in a sealed freezer-weight container, leave it in hot water until the food separates from its sides. Open the bag or container; invert contents into a saucepan.

To thaw casseroles: At least 24 hours but no more than 2 days before reheating, refrigerate the frozen casserole to thaw slightly. If the casserole was frozen in a foil-lined baking dish and then removed from the dish for storage, unwrap it and slip it back into the baking dish to thaw.

To reheat soups and stews: Add ¼ to ½ cup *water* to the saucepan to prevent scorching. Cover and heat to boiling over medium heat, stirring frequently, then boil 1 minute to be sure it's fully heated.

To reheat casseroles: Unwrap the frozen casserole; loosely cover it with foil, and bake about 1 hour at the temperature specified in the recipe, then uncover and bake 20 to 30 minutes longer or until the center of the casserole reaches 160°F on an instant-read thermometer.

SCRUMPTIOUS MAINS

To make skinny meal-planning a cinch, each of our comforting main dishes is paired with suggestions for add-on recipes that will make it a meal. Or to choose your own add-ons, see the complete recipe lists in the second half of the book, conveniently organized by calorie count, from lowest to highest: Potatoes, Breads & Stuffings, page 111; Veggies & Side Salads, page 125; and Sweet Finales, page 137.

290
CALORIES
Classic Beef Stew
(page 32)

SUPER SLOW COOKING

Nothing is more comforting on a cold day than a bowl of soup or stew. Here we offer lots of hearty options, all slow simmered on the stovetop or in a slow cooker for maximum convenience. (See "The Skinny on Slow Cooking" on page 14 for tips.) Fill your soup pot with classic soups like French onion, chicken noodle, fish chowder, and gumbo, each for 400 calories or less per serving. Or use your slow cooker to make satisfying stews or meat dishes ranging from coq au vin and chili to ribs and pulled pork.

KEY TO ICONS

⏱ 30 minutes or less   ♥ Heart healthy   🌾 High fiber   🍲 Make ahead   🍲 Slow cooker

FRENCH ONION SOUP

Everyone loves the gooey richness of French onion soup—but not the excess fat and salt. So we swapped in olive oil for butter and added a dash of soy sauce to chicken broth to mimic the savory depth of salty beef stock. Finally, we blanketed our dish with Gruyère and reduced-fat Swiss—because what's onion soup without the cheese?

ACTIVE TIME: 20 MINUTES · TOTAL TIME: 1 HOUR

MAKES: 4 MAIN-DISH SERVINGS

1   TABLESPOON EXTRA-VIRGIN OLIVE OIL

3   LARGE RED ONIONS (12 OUNCES EACH), VERY THINLY SLICED

3   SPRIGS FRESH THYME

½   TEASPOON SALT

½   CUP DRY RED WINE

1   CAN (14½ OUNCES) REDUCED-SODIUM CHICKEN BROTH

2¼ CUPS WATER

2   TEASPOONS REDUCED-SODIUM SOY SAUCE

4   SLICES WHOLE-WHEAT BAGUETTE (½ INCH THICK)

1   TEASPOON CORNSTARCH

½   TEASPOON GROUND BLACK PEPPER

1¼ OUNCES SHREDDED GRUYÈRE CHEESE (5 TABLESPOONS)

4   SLICES REDUCED-FAT SWISS CHEESE

1   In 5-quart Dutch oven or heavy saucepot, heat oil on medium-high. Stir in onions, thyme, and ¼ teaspoon salt; cover partially. Cook 15 to 17 minutes or until onions are golden brown and very tender, stirring occasionally.
2   Add wine and simmer 2 to 4 minutes or until reduced by half. Add broth, water, and soy sauce. Heat to boiling on high, then reduce heat to maintain a gentle simmer; simmer 20 minutes.
3   Arrange oven rack 6 inches from broiler heat source and preheat broiler. Place bread slices in jelly-roll pan. Broil 30 to 60 seconds or until golden brown. Divide among 8-ounce ovenproof soup crocks or ramekins.
4   In small bowl, stir cornstarch and 1 tablespoon soup liquid from pot until cornstarch dissolves. Stir into soup and simmer 2 minutes. Stir in pepper and remaining ¼ teaspoon salt. Discard thyme. Divide soup among soup crocks.
5   Sprinkle Gruyère evenly over soup, then place 1 slice Swiss on top of each crock. Broil 1 to 2 minutes or until golden brown on top. Serve hot.

260
CALORIES

PER SERVING. 14G PROTEIN | 30G CARBOHYDRATE | 11G TOTAL FAT (4G SATURATED) 5G FIBER | 20MG CHOLESTEROL | 650MG SODIUM

MAKE IT A MEAL: Pair with a whole-grain roll (75 calories) and a crisp green salad with 2 tablespoons low-fat dressing (75 calories) for added fiber—and 410 calories total.

HEARTY FISH CHOWDER

Cod, bacon, and potatoes make this creamy chowder rich and satisfying.
Reduced-fat milk keeps the calories in check.

ACTIVE TIME: 20 MINUTES · TOTAL TIME: 35 MINUTES

MAKES: 4 MAIN-DISH SERVINGS

4   SLICES CENTER-CUT BACON

1   LARGE CARROT, CHOPPED

1   (13-OUNCE) CELERY ROOT (CELERIAC), PEELED AND CHOPPED

1   LARGE ALL-PURPOSE POTATO, PEELED AND CHOPPED

2   TABLESPOONS PLUS ½ CUP WATER

2   SMALL ONIONS, CHOPPED

2   TABLESPOONS ALL-PURPOSE FLOUR

1   CUP CLAM JUICE, BOTTLED

1   POUND SKINLESS COD FILLETS, CUT INTO 1-INCH CHUNKS

½   CUP REDUCED-FAT MILK (2%)

¼   TEASPOON SALT

⅛   TEASPOON GROUND BLACK PEPPER

FRESH FLAT-LEAF PARSLEY LEAVES, CHOPPED, FOR GARNISH

1   In 6- to 7-quart saucepot, cook bacon on medium 5 to 7 minutes or until browned and crisp, turning occasionally. Drain on paper towels; set aside and crumble when cooled. Discard all but 1 tablespoon bacon fat.

2   While bacon cooks, in large microwave-safe bowl, combine carrot, celery root, potato, and 2 tablespoons water. Cover with vented plastic wrap and microwave on High 5 minutes or until vegetables are just tender.

3   Keep saucepot with rendered bacon fat on medium. Add onions and cook 6 to 8 minutes or until tender, stirring occasionally. Add carrot mixture and cook 2 minutes, stirring.

4   Add flour; cook 2 minutes, stirring. Add clam juice and ½ cup water; whisk until smooth. Heat to boiling, stirring often. Add cod chunks, cover, and cook 4 to 5 minutes or until fish just turns opaque throughout.

5   Stir in milk, salt, and pepper. Cook 1 to 2 minutes or until hot but not boiling. Spoon chowder into shallow bowls; garnish with parsley and crumbled bacon.

310 CALORIES **PER SERVING.** 27G PROTEIN | 35G CARBOHYDRATE | 7G TOTAL FAT (3G SATURATED) 5G FIBER | 64MG CHOLESTEROL | 595MG SODIUM ✿

MAKE IT A MEAL: For a 410-calorie lunch, add on half a mini pita stuffed with 2 tablespoons each mashed avocado and chopped tomato (100 calories).

SWEET POTATO SOUP

Sweet potatoes, loaded with vitamin A in the form of beta-carotene, form the base of this hearty, vivid orange soup. Avocado adds healthy, skin-softening fats, which also aid the body's absorption of beta-carotene.

ACTIVE TIME: 25 MINUTES · TOTAL TIME: 45 MINUTES
MAKES: 6 MAIN-DISH SERVINGS

2   TABLESPOONS OLIVE OIL

1   ONION, FINELY CHOPPED

1   RED PEPPER, FINELY CHOPPED

3   GARLIC CLOVES, FINELY CHOPPED

1½ TEASPOONS GROUND CUMIN

½   TEASPOON SMOKED PAPRIKA

¼   TEASPOON GROUND CINNAMON

1   TEASPOON SALT

1   CARTON (32 OUNCES) REDUCED-SODIUM VEGETABLE BROTH

2   POUNDS SWEET POTATOES, PEELED AND CUT INTO ½-INCH CHUNKS

2   CANS (15 OUNCES EACH) REDUCED-SODIUM BLACK BEANS, RINSED AND DRAINED

2   CUPS WATER

¼   TEASPOON GROUND BLACK PEPPER

1   HASS AVOCADO, THINLY SLICED

¼   CUP PACKED FRESH CILANTRO LEAVES

1   LIME, CUT INTO WEDGES

1   In 5- to 6-quart saucepot, heat oil on medium. Add onion and red pepper; cook 5 minutes, stirring. Stir in garlic, cumin, paprika, cinnamon, and ½ teaspoon salt. Cook 2 minutes, stirring.

2   Add broth, potatoes, beans, water, and black pepper. Heat to boiling on high. Reduce heat to medium; simmer 15 minutes.

3   Transfer 3 cups of soup to blender. Puree until smooth; return to pot. Stir in remaining ½ teaspoon salt. Serve, garnished with avocado, cilantro, and lime wedges.

330 CALORIES

PER SERVING. 11G PROTEIN | 53G CARBOHYDRATE | 8G TOTAL FAT (1G SATURATED) 13G FIBER | 0MG CHOLESTEROL | 600MG SODIUM 🌱 📷

MAKE IT A MEAL: For a 505-calorie dinner, serve with a square of our Golden Corn Bread (175 calories; page 119). This meal is great for busy weeknights and for a casual dinner with friends, too.

SHRIMP AND SAUSAGE GUMBO

This spicy Cajun creation features succulent fresh shrimp, tender Italian sausage, and plenty of veggies, making this one-pot dinner as nutritious as it is delicious.

ACTIVE TIME: 40 MINUTES · TOTAL TIME: 1 HOUR
MAKES: 10 MAIN-DISH SERVINGS

---

1   POUND HOT ITALIAN SAUSAGE LINKS, PRICKED SEVERAL TIMES WITH FORK

3   TABLESPOONS VEGETABLE OIL

¼   CUP ALL-PURPOSE FLOUR

1   GREEN PEPPER, CHOPPED

1   ONION, CHOPPED

2   STALKS CELERY, CHOPPED

2   GARLIC CLOVES, FINELY CHOPPED

1   CAN (14½ OUNCES) CHICKEN BROTH

1   CAN (14½ OUNCES) STEWED TOMATOES

1   CUP WATER

1   PACKAGE (10 OUNCES) FROZEN SLICED OKRA, THAWED

1   BAY LEAF

¼   TEASPOON DRIED OREGANO

¼   TEASPOON DRIED THYME

½   TEASPOON SALT

1½ CUPS REGULAR LONG-GRAIN WHITE RICE

1½ POUNDS SHELLED AND DEVEINED SHRIMP, WITH TAIL PART OF SHELL LEFT ON IF YOU LIKE

1   Heat 6-quart Dutch oven on medium-high until hot. Add sausage links and cook 8 minutes or until well browned, turning frequently. Transfer sausages to plate to cool slightly, about 10 minutes. When cool, cut sausages into ½-inch-thick diagonal slices.

2   While sausages cool, discard all but 1 tablespoon drippings from Dutch oven. Add oil to Dutch oven and heat on medium. (If your sausages are very lean and you do not get 1 tablespoon drippings, add enough additional oil to drippings to equal ¼ cup fat total.) Gradually stir flour into drippings until blended, and cook 4 to 5 minutes or until flour mixture (roux) is deep brown, stirring constantly. Add green pepper, onion, celery, and garlic and cook 5 to 6 minutes or until all vegetables are tender, stirring occasionally.

3   Return sausages to Dutch oven; stir in broth, tomatoes, water, okra, bay leaf, oregano, thyme, and ¼ teaspoon salt; heat to boiling on high. Reduce heat to low; cover and simmer 30 minutes to blend flavors.

4   Meanwhile, prepare rice as label directs. In medium bowl, toss shrimp with remaining ¼ teaspoon salt.

5 Add shrimp to Dutch oven; cook 2 to 3 minutes or until opaque throughout.

6 To serve, discard bay leaf. Serve gumbo in large bowls. Top each serving with a scoop of rice.

400
CALORIES **PER SERVING.** 25G PROTEIN | 33G CARBOHYDRATE | 17G TOTAL FAT (5G SATURATED) 3G FIBER | 135MG CHOLESTEROL | 680MG SODIUM

MAKE IT A MEAL: Enjoy a Chocolate Chip–Oatmeal Cookie (80 calories; page 139) for dessert, if you like. The entire meal will cost you just 480 calories.

CHICKEN NOODLE SOUP

For classic comfort food, nothing beats chicken noodle soup. And this slow-cooker recipe is almost effortless—the whole bird is slow-poached on top of vegetables, creating a delicious, rich broth. For photo, see page 6.

ACTIVE TIME: 20 MINUTES · SLOW-COOK TIME: 8 HOURS 20 MINUTES ON LOW OR 4 HOURS 20 MINUTES ON HIGH

MAKES: 14 CUPS OR 6 MAIN-DISH SERVINGS

8 CUPS WATER	½ TEASPOON DRIED THYME
4 CARROTS, CUT INTO ¼-INCH SLICES	1 TABLESPOON SALT
4 STALKS CELERY, CUT INTO ¼-INCH SLICES	½ TEASPOON GROUND BLACK PEPPER
1 SMALL ONION, CHOPPED	1 WHOLE CHICKEN (3½ POUNDS)
2 BAY LEAVES	3 CUPS EGG NOODLES, UNCOOKED

1 In 4½- to 6-quart slow-cooker bowl, combine water, carrots, celery, onion, bay leaves, thyme, salt, and pepper. Place whole chicken on top of vegetables. Cover slow cooker with lid and cook as manufacturer directs on Low 8 to 10 hours or on High 4 to 5 hours.

2 Transfer chicken to cutting board. Discard bay leaves. Add noodles to slow-cooker bowl; cover with lid and cook (on Low or High) 20 minutes.

3 While noodles cook, remove and discard skin, fat, and bones from chicken; shred meat.

4 Skim fat from soup and discard. Return chicken to soup to serve.

315 CALORIES

PER SERVING. 33G PROTEIN | 26G CARBOHYDRATE | 8G TOTAL FAT (2G SATURATED) 3G FIBER | 112MG CHOLESTEROL | 1,385MG SODIUM

MAKE IT A MEAL: Enjoy everyone's favorite soup the classic way—with two squares of Saltines (26 calories total) crumbled on top. Add ten baby carrots (40 calories) on the side for a 380-calorie lunch.

EIGHT-HOUR COQ AU VIN

We removed the skin from the chicken to cut back on calories and fat.

ACTIVE TIME: 20 MINUTES · SLOW-COOK TIME: 8 HOURS ON LOW OR 4 HOURS ON HIGH
MAKES: 4 MAIN-DISH SERVINGS

3   SLICES BACON, CUT CROSSWISE INTO ¾-INCH PIECES

10 OUNCES MUSHROOMS, EACH CUT IN HALF

2   CUPS FROZEN PEARL ONIONS

1   CUT-UP CHICKEN (3½ TO 4 POUNDS), SKIN REMOVED FROM ALL PIECES EXCEPT WINGS

½   TEASPOON SALT

¼   TEASPOON GROUND BLACK PEPPER

1   ONION, CHOPPED

1   LARGE CARROT, PEELED AND CHOPPED

4   GARLIC CLOVES, CHOPPED

1   CUP DRY RED WINE

2   TABLESPOONS TOMATO PASTE

1   BAY LEAF

¾   CUP CANNED CHICKEN BROTH

1 In nonstick 12-inch skillet, cook bacon over medium heat until browned. With slotted spoon, transfer bacon to paper towels to drain; refrigerate.

2 Meanwhile, in 5- to 6-quart slow-cooker bowl, combine mushrooms and pearl onions.

3 Sprinkle chicken pieces with salt and pepper. In skillet with bacon fat, brown chicken (in two batches, if necessary) over medium-high heat, about 10 minutes. Place chicken over vegetables in slow cooker.

4 Discard drippings from skillet. Reduce heat to medium; add chopped onion and carrot and cook, stirring frequently, until onion softens, about 2 minutes. Stir in garlic and cook 1 minute. Add wine, tomato paste, and bay leaf; heat to boiling, stirring to blend in tomato paste. Pour wine mixture and broth over chicken. Cover slow cooker and cook on Low 8 hours or on High 4 hours.

5 To serve, discard bay leaf. With large spoon, transfer chicken and sauce to deep platter; sprinkle with bacon.

400 CALORIES

PER SERVING. 52G PROTEIN | 20G CARBOHYDRATE | 13G TOTAL FAT (4G SATURATED) 5G FIBER | 156MG CHOLESTEROL | 690MG SODIUM

MAKE IT A MEAL: Enjoy this classic on its own or add a frosted Brownie Bite (100 calories; page 141) for dessert. The total calorie count: 500.

A PERFECT POT OF RICE

If you'd like to serve this chicken dish over rice, follow these tips to ensure the grains are tender (not sticky or crunchy!).

• There's no need to rinse domestic white rice before cooking, but you should rinse imported varieties such as basmati or jasmine, which may be dirty or dusty. Place the rice in a sieve, then place the sieve in a bowl of cold water and swish it back and forth. Lift out the sieve, pour off the water, and repeat until the water looks clear.

• The general rule of thumb when cooking rice is 2 cups of water or other liquid to 1 cup of rice, but follow the instructions on the package for exact liquid measurements and estimated cooking times. Be sure to allow the rice to steam with the lid on as the package instructs; any remaining water will be absorbed, ensuring tender rice.

• Add salt to the rice at the beginning of the cook time; don't try tossing it in at the end! Typically ¼ teaspoon salt per 1 cup rice is suggested, but follow the instructions provided on the rice package.

RED-COOKED CHICKEN WITH VEGGIES

A sweet and spicy glaze coats this richly hued, Asian-style chicken, which practically falls off the bone, thanks to the gentle, slow cooking. A bag of fresh mixed vegetables are stirred in at the last minute—an easy way to add color and essential nutrients.

ACTIVE TIME: 20 MINUTES · SLOW-COOK TIME: 8 HOURS ON LOW OR 4 HOURS ON HIGH
MAKES: 4 MAIN-DISH SERVINGS

1 BUNCH GREEN ONIONS	3 GARLIC CLOVES, CRUSHED WITH GARLIC PRESS
½ CUP DRY SHERRY	
⅓ CUP SOY SAUCE	3 POUNDS SKINLESS, BONE-IN CHICKEN THIGHS
¼ CUP PACKED BROWN SUGAR	
2 TABLESPOONS GRATED, PEELED FRESH GINGER	1 BAG (16 OUNCES) MIXED FRESH VEGGIES FOR STIR-FRY (SUCH AS SNOW PEAS, CARROTS, BROCCOLI, AND RED PEPPER)
1 TEASPOON CHINESE FIVE-SPICE POWDER	

1 Cut green onions into 2-inch pieces and place white parts in 5- to 6-quart slow cooker; coarsely chop remaining green parts, wrap, and refrigerate until serving time. To onions in slow cooker, add sherry, soy sauce, sugar, ginger, five-spice powder, and garlic. Add chicken thighs and coat with sherry mixture. Cover slow cooker and cook as manufacturer directs, on Low 8 hours or on High 4 hours.

2 Just before serving, place vegetables in microwave-safe medium bowl and cook in microwave as label directs.

3 With tongs, transfer chicken to deep platter. Stir vegetables into slow cooker. Spoon vegetable mixture around chicken. Sprinkle with reserved chopped green onions.

355 CALORIES

PER SERVING. 43G PROTEIN | 27G CARBOHYDRATE | 8G TOTAL FAT (2G SATURATED) 4G FIBER | 161MG CHOLESTEROL | 1,515MG SODIUM

MAKE IT A MEAL: Enjoy this ample chicken and vegetable stew on its own, or serve it over ¾ cup aromatic jasmine or basmati rice (155 calories) for an easy 510-calorie dinner.

CHIPOTLE BEEF CHILI

This super-satisfying main dish is perfect for potlucks and other casual parties. The chili can be made a day ahead and refrigerated. To reheat, transfer it to a Dutch oven and heat it on medium until it comes to a simmer; reduce the heat to low, cover, and simmer 20 minutes to heat through.

ACTIVE TIME: 25 MINUTES · SLOW-COOK TIME: 6 HOURS ON HIGH
MAKES: 10 MAIN-DISH SERVINGS

2   CANS (15 TO 19 OUNCES) BEANS, PREFERABLY BLACK PLUS PINTO OR RED BEANS

1   CAN (7 OUNCES) CHIPOTLE CHILES IN ADOBO

1   CAN (28 OUNCES) DICED FIRE-ROASTED TOMATOES

1   LARGE ONION (10 TO 12 OUNCES), FINELY CHOPPED

1   MEDIUM GREEN PEPPER (6 TO 8 OUNCES), FINELY CHOPPED

2   GARLIC CLOVES, CRUSHED WITH GARLIC PRESS

2½ POUNDS BEEF CHUCK, CUT INTO 1-INCH CHUNKS

1   TABLESPOON GROUND CUMIN

½   TABLESPOON DRIED OREGANO

⅛   TEASPOON SALT

⅛   TEASPOON GROUND BLACK PEPPER

2   OUNCES MONTEREY JACK CHEESE, SHREDDED (½ CUP)

½   CUP REDUCED-FAT SOUR CREAM

½   CUP PACKED FRESH CILANTRO LEAVES, COARSELY CHOPPED

1   LIME, CUT INTO WEDGES

1   In large colander, drain beans. Rinse well and drain again. Remove 1 chile from can of chipotle chiles in adobo and finely chop. Place in large bowl with 1 teaspoon adobo. Reserve another 2 teaspoons adobo for cooked chili, and reserve remaining chiles and adobo for another use.

2   To large bowl with chiles and adobo, add tomatoes, onions, green peppers, and garlic; mix well. In another large bowl, combine beef, cumin, oregano, salt, and pepper.

3   In 7-quart slow-cooker bowl, spread a generous layer of tomato mixture. Add beef, then beans to slow-cooker bowl and top with remaining tomato mixture. Cover slow cooker with lid and cook as manufacturer directs on High setting 6 hours.

4 Using slotted spoon, transfer solids to large serving bowl. Transfer cooking liquid from slow-cooker bowl to 4-cup liquid measuring cup. Remove and discard fat. Pour off all but 2 cups cooking liquid. Stir reserved adobo into cooking liquid in cup; pour over chili and stir to combine. Serve with Monterey Jack, sour cream, cilantro, and limes alongside.

325 CALORIES

PER SERVING. 32G PROTEIN | 23G CARBOHYDRATE | 12G TOTAL FAT (5G SATURATED) 7G FIBER | 71MG CHOLESTEROL | 515MG SODIUM

MAKE IT A MEAL: Start off with Slimmed-Down Potato Skins (120 calories per serving; page 116). Or pair with a slice of our Golden Corn Bread (175 calories; page 119) for a 500-calorie meal.

CLASSIC BEEF STEW

Be sure to trim excess fat from the chuck to keep both calories and saturated fat in check. For photo, see page 18.

ACTIVE TIME: 45 MINUTES · TOTAL TIME: 2 HOURS 45 MINUTES

MAKES: 8 MAIN-DISH SERVINGS

- 2 POUNDS BONELESS BEEF CHUCK, TRIMMED OF FAT AND CUT INTO 1½-INCH PIECES
- 4 TEASPOONS OLIVE OIL
- 1 LARGE ONION (12 OUNCES), CHOPPED
- 2 GARLIC CLOVES, FINELY CHOPPED
- 1 CAN (14 OUNCES) DICED TOMATOES
- 2 CUPS DRY RED WINE
- 1 BAY LEAF

- 1 TEASPOON SALT
- ¼ TEASPOON GROUND BLACK PEPPER
- ¼ TEASPOON DRIED THYME
- 1½ POUNDS POTATOES, PEELED AND CUT INTO 1½-INCH PIECES
- 6 CARROTS, PEELED AND CUT INTO 1-INCH PIECES
- 1 CUP FROZEN PEAS
- 2 TABLESPOONS CHOPPED FRESH PARSLEY LEAVES

1   Preheat oven to 325°F. Pat beef dry with paper towels. In 6-quart Dutch oven, heat 2 teaspoons oil over medium-high heat until very hot. Add half of beef and cook 5 minutes or until well browned on all sides. Transfer beef to large bowl. Add remaining 2 teaspoons oil to Dutch oven and repeat with remaining beef.

2   Reduce heat to medium. Add onion to pot and cook, stirring occasionally, until tender, about 5 minutes. Add garlic and cook 30 seconds or until very fragrant. Stir in tomatoes with their juices. Add wine, bay leaf, salt, pepper, thyme, and beef with its accumulated juices. Heat to boiling over high heat. Cover and transfer to oven. Cook 1 hour. Add potatoes and carrots; cook 1 hour longer or until vegetables are fork-tender. Discard bay leaf.

3   With slotted spoon, transfer vegetables and beef to bowl and cover with foil to keep warm. Skim and discard fat from cooking liquid.

4   Raise heat to medium-high and cook liquid until slightly reduced, 5 to 7 minutes. Stir in frozen peas and cook 1 to 2 minutes longer or until heated through. Spoon liquid and peas over meat mixture. Sprinkle with parsley.

290 CALORIES

PER SERVING. 27G PROTEIN | 2G CARBOHYDRATE | 7G TOTAL FAT (2G SATURATED) 5G FIBER | 48MG CHOLESTEROL | 450MG SODIUM ♥ ❂ ☷

MAKE IT A MEAL: Serve with Golden Corn Muffins (145 calories; page 119) on the side for a comforting 435-calorie family-style meal.

LOW-AND-SLOW RIBS WITH ASIAN CUKE SALAD

These Asian-style ribs are paired with a refreshing carrot and cucumber slaw. You'll need eight hours to slow-cook the pork spareribs (on Low), but the reward for your patience is delectable.

ACTIVE TIME: 20 MINUTES · SLOW-COOK TIME: 8 HOURS ON LOW OR 4 HOURS ON HIGH
MAKES: 8 MAIN-DISH SERVINGS

3½ POUNDS PORK SPARERIBS

1 CUP TERIYAKI GLAZE (SEE TIP)

1 (12 TO 14 OUNCES) ENGLISH (SEEDLESS) CUCUMBER, PEELED AND THINLY SLICED

1 BAG (10 OUNCES) SHREDDED CARROTS

¼ CUP SEASONED RICE VINEGAR

1   In 4½- to 6-quart slow-cooker bowl, place ribs and teriyaki glaze, spreading teriyaki to coat ribs on all sides. Cover slow cooker with lid and cook as manufacturer directs on Low 8 hours or on High 4 hours.

2   Meanwhile, in medium bowl, stir cucumber, carrots, and rice vinegar until blended. Cover and refrigerate until ready to serve. Makes about 4 cups salad.

3   To serve, transfer ribs to cutting board; cut into portions. Skim and discard fat from cooking liquid. Arrange ribs and salad on dinner plates. Spoon remaining liquid over ribs.

TIP We got luscious stick-to-the-ribs results using a thick teriyaki glaze (such as Kikkoman's Teriyaki Baste & Glaze) rather than a thinner sauce.

390 CALORIES

PER SERVING. 26G PROTEIN | 18G CARBOHYDRATE | 22G TOTAL FAT (9G SATURATED) 1G FIBER | 89MG CHOLESTEROL | 1,185MG SODIUM

MAKE IT A MEAL: Start the meal with ½ cup steamed edamame beans (100 calories) for a better-than-takeout 490-calorie meal.

PULLED PORK SANDWICHES

The prep on this slow-cooked dish takes about ten minutes. For a stress-free morning, rub the pork and combine sauce ingredients the night before, then place them in your slow cooker in the morning. Transfer any leftovers to airtight containers, then label and freeze them for up to three months.

TOTAL TIME: 8 HOURS 30 MINUTES

MAKES: 16 SANDWICHES

- 2 TABLESPOONS SMOKED PAPRIKA
- 1 TABLESPOON MUSTARD POWDER
- ¼ CUP PLUS 1 TABLESPOON PACKED DARK BROWN SUGAR
- 2 TEASPOONS SALT
- 2 TEASPOONS GROUND BLACK PEPPER
- 4 POUNDS BONELESS, UNTRIMMED PORK SHOULDER BLADE ROAST (BOSTON BUTT)
- 1 CUP CIDER VINEGAR
- ½ CUP KETCHUP
- 2 TEASPOONS CRUSHED RED PEPPER
- 1 CUP WATER
- 2 TABLESPOONS LIGHT MAYONNAISE
- 2 BAGS (14 OUNCES EACH) COLESLAW MIX
- 16 SOFT WHITE HAMBURGER BUNS, LIGHTLY TOASTED

1 In 5- to 6-quart slow-cooker bowl, combine paprika, mustard powder, ¼ cup brown sugar, 1 teaspoon salt, and 1 teaspoon pepper. Add pork and rub mixture all over meat. Arrange pork in single layer in slow-cooker bowl, fat side up.

2 In medium bowl, whisk vinegar, ketchup, red pepper, remaining 1 teaspoon each salt and pepper, and remaining 1 tablespoon brown sugar. Pour ⅓ cup sauce into large bowl; cover and refrigerate. Pour water and remaining sauce into slow-cooker bowl. Cover slow cooker with lid, and cook as manufacturer directs on Low 8 to 10 hours, or until meat is fork-tender.

3 Carefully transfer meat to large bowl; remove fat and skin and discard. Using two forks, shred meat into small pieces. Carefully pour sauce from slow cooker into fat separator. Pour half of sauce over meat and pour remaining sauce into gravy boat. Discard fat.

4 When ready to serve, remove reserved sauce from refrigerator; with fork, whisk in mayonnaise. Add coleslaw mix, and toss until well combined. Divide meat among bottoms of buns; top with coleslaw, then tops of buns. Serve with reserved sauce alongside.

385 CALORIES

PER SANDWICH. 32G PROTEIN | 33G CARBOHYDRATE | 14G TOTAL FAT (4G SATURATED) | 3G FIBER | 98MG CHOLESTEROL | 595MG SODIUM

MAKE IT A MEAL: This main dish includes a quick coleslaw. For a 515-calorie BBQ-style dinner, add on Corn on the Cob with Spicy Butter (130 calories; page 132).

395
CALORIES
Smothered Pork Chops
(page 52)

FAST WEEKNIGHT FAVES

Your family is sure to love these quick and delicious low-calorie meals, which we hope will become standbys in your weeknight dinner repertoire. Enjoy easy skillet dishes like Apricot-Glazed Chicken, Chicken-Fried Steak, and Smothered Pork Chops—all three include tasty sides you make in the same pan as the main dish. Or try lighter oven-baked versions of typically deep-fried dishes, including our kid-friendly Oven-Fried Chicken Tenders with a zippy barbecue sauce and Island-Spiced Fish Sticks dipped in a spicy lime mayonnaise.

KEY TO ICONS

⌄ 30 minutes or less   ♥ Heart healthy   ⊛ High fiber   ▦ Make ahead   ▢ Slow cooker

OVEN-FRIED CHICKEN TENDERS WITH FIVE-SPICE BBQ SAUCE

Chicken tenders are dipped in egg white, lightly breaded with panko and sesame seeds, and then baked to keep calories and fat in check. Five-spice powder and a little brown sugar make the barbecue sauce delectable.

ACTIVE TIME: 10 MINUTES · TOTAL TIME: 30 MINUTES
MAKES: 4 MAIN-DISH SERVINGS

¾ CUP PANKO (JAPANESE-STYLE BREAD CRUMBS)

2 TABLESPOONS SESAME SEEDS

1 LARGE EGG WHITE

1 TEASPOON CHINESE FIVE-SPICE POWDER

½ TEASPOON SALT

1 POUND CHICKEN BREAST TENDERS

1 TABLESPOON OLIVE OIL

1 SMALL ONION, CHOPPED

½ CUP KETCHUP

1 TABLESPOON BROWN SUGAR

1½ TEASPOONS CIDER VINEGAR

1½ TEASPOONS WORCESTERSHIRE SAUCE

1 Preheat oven to 475°F. In 10-inch skillet, toast bread crumbs and sesame seeds over high heat, stirring frequently, until golden, about 5 minutes. Transfer crumb mixture to plate. Do not wash skillet.

2 In medium bowl, with wire whisk or fork, mix egg white, ½ teaspoon five-spice powder, and salt until foamy. Dip chicken tenders in egg-white mixture, then in crumb mixture to coat. Place tenders on cookie sheet and bake, without turning, until they lose their pink color throughout, 13 to 15 minutes.

3 Meanwhile, in same skillet, heat oil over medium heat until hot. Add onion and cook until soft and lightly browned, 8 to 10 minutes. Remove skillet from heat; stir in ketchup, brown sugar, vinegar, Worcestershire, and remaining ½ teaspoon five-spice powder. Pour sauce into small bowl and serve with tenders.

280 CALORIES **PER SERVING.** 30G PROTEIN | 23G CARBOHYDRATE | 8G TOTAL FAT (1G SATURATED) 1G FIBER | 66MG CHOLESTEROL | 775MG SODIUM 🗸

MAKE IT A MEAL: Serve with Oven Fries (130 calories; page 118) baked along-side the chicken at 475°F for an easy 410-calorie meal.

APRICOT-GLAZED CHICKEN

Quick-cooking and healthy spinach makes this scrumptious glazed chicken recipe an easy weeknight option.

TOTAL TIME: 30 MINUTES

MAKES: 4 MAIN-DISH SERVINGS

4 MEDIUM SKINLESS, BONELESS CHICKEN-BREAST HALVES (1½ POUNDS)

⅜ TEASPOON SALT

¼ TEASPOON GROUND BLACK PEPPER

4 TEASPOONS OLIVE OIL

1 LEMON

1 SMALL ONION, CHOPPED

⅓ CUP APRICOT PRESERVES

⅓ CUP CANNED CHICKEN BROTH

1 TABLESPOON DIJON MUSTARD

1 PACKAGE (9 OUNCES) MICROWAVE-IN-THE-BAG SPINACH

1   With meat mallet, pound chicken placed between two sheets waxed paper or plastic wrap to even ½-inch thickness; season with ¼ teaspoon salt and ⅛ teaspoon pepper.

2   In 12-inch skillet, heat 2 teaspoons oil on medium until hot. Add chicken and cook 6 to 8 minutes or until browned on both sides, turning over once. Transfer chicken to dish. Meanwhile, from lemon, grate ½ teaspoon peel and squeeze 1 tablespoon juice; set aside.

3   To same skillet, heat remaining 2 teaspoons oil on medium until hot. Add onion and cook 6 minutes or until tender. Add preserves, broth, mustard, and lemon peel; heat to boiling on medium-high. Boil 1 minute. Return chicken to skillet; reduce heat to medium-low and simmer 4 to 6 minutes, spooning preserve mixture over breasts frequently, until chicken is glazed and instant-read thermometer inserted sideways into center of cutlets registers 165°F.

4   Meanwhile, cook spinach as label directs. Transfer to serving bowl and toss with lemon juice and remaining ⅛ teaspoon each salt and pepper. Serve spinach with chicken; spoon any extra preserve mixture over chicken.

325 CALORIES   **PER SERVING.** 42G PROTEIN | 22G CARBOHYDRATE | 7G TOTAL FAT (1G SATURATED) 7G FIBER | 99MG CHOLESTEROL | 480MG SODIUM ♥ ♥ ✿

MAKE IT A MEAL: Serve with a side of steamed red potatoes (100 calories for one medium potato) for a comforting 425-calorie dinner.

CHICKEN-FRIED STEAK

Whole-wheat flour, reduced-fat milk, and canola oil (instead of lard or bacon fat) makes this recipe for Southern chicken-fried steak just a little bit healthier. For photo, see page 11.

ACTIVE TIME: 30 MINUTES · **TOTAL TIME:** 35 MINUTES
MAKES: 4 MAIN-DISH SERVINGS

1 CUP WHITE WHOLE-WHEAT OR WHOLE-WHEAT FLOUR

½ TEASPOON CAYENNE (GROUND RED) PEPPER

⅝ TEASPOON SALT

1 TEASPOON PEPPER

1 LARGE EGG WHITE

1 CUP PLUS 2 TABLESPOONS REDUCED-FAT MILK (2%)

1 POUND SANDWICH-CUT BEEF STEAKS (EACH ¼ INCH THICK)

4 TABLESPOONS CANOLA OIL

1 On plate, combine flour, cayenne, and ½ teaspoon each salt and black pepper. Set 2 tablespoons mixture aside.

2 In shallow dish, beat egg white and 2 tablespoons milk until frothy.

3 Dip 1 steak in flour mixture; shake off excess, then dip in egg mixture and let excess drip off. Dip in flour mixture again until coated; transfer to waxed paper–lined plate. Repeat with remaining steaks.

4 In 12-inch skillet, heat 3 tablespoons oil on medium-high until shimmering. Shake excess flour off 1 steak; carefully add to hot oil. Cook 2 to 4 minutes or until golden brown on both sides, turning over once. Transfer to paper towels. Reheat oil; add another steak. Repeat until all steaks are cooked. Pour off fat from skillet; discard. Wipe out skillet.

5 In skillet, heat remaining 1 tablespoon oil on medium-low. Whisk in reserved flour mixture. Cook 1 minute or until fragrant, whisking. Gradually whisk in remaining 1 cup milk. Heat to boiling on medium, then cook 2 minutes or until thickened, whisking. Whisk in remaining ⅛ teaspoon salt and ½ teaspoon black pepper. Serve with steaks.

390 CALORIES **PER SERVING.** 35G PROTEIN | 19G CARBOHYDRATE | 19G TOTAL FAT (4G SATURATED) 1G FIBER | 92MG CHOLESTEROL | 465MG SODIUM ♥

MAKE IT A MEAL: For a soul-satisfying 485-calorie supper, serve our Parmesan-cheese-topped Broccoli Gratin (95 calories; page 131) on the side.

ISLAND-SPICED FISH STICKS

Turn cod fillets into spicy fish sticks, using thyme, allspice, a jalapeño chile pepper, and a coating of panko bread crumbs.

ACTIVE TIME: 20 MINUTES · **TOTAL TIME:** 30 MINUTES PLUS CHILLING
MAKES: 4 MAIN-DISH SERVINGS

NONSTICK OLIVE OIL COOKING SPRAY

2 LIMES

2 GREEN ONIONS, LIGHT AND DARK GREEN PARTS ONLY

¼ CUP PACKED FRESH PARSLEY LEAVES

½ JALAPEÑO CHILE, SEEDS REMOVED

1 TEASPOON FRESH THYME LEAVES

¼ TEASPOON GROUND ALLSPICE

⅝ TEASPOON SALT

1 LARGE EGG WHITE

1 POUND SKINLESS COD FILLET

¾ CUP PANKO (JAPANESE-STYLE BREAD CRUMBS)

2 TABLESPOONS LIGHT MAYONNAISE

2 TABLESPOONS REDUCED-FAT SOUR CREAM

1 BAG (5 TO 6 OUNCES) BABY SPINACH

1   Lightly coat cookie sheet with nonstick cooking spray. Cut 1 lime into wedges and set aside until ready to serve. From remaining lime, grate 1 teaspoon peel and squeeze 2 teaspoons juice. In small bowl, place juice and ½ teaspoon peel. Finely chop 1 tablespoon green onion and add to bowl with lime juice; set aside. Cut remaining green onions into large pieces.

2   In food processor with knife blade attached, place parsley, jalapeño, thyme, allspice, green onion pieces, ½ teaspoon salt, and remaining ½ teaspoon lime peel. Pulse until finely chopped.

3   In medium bowl, lightly beat egg white. Remove any bones from cod and cut cod into 2-inch chunks. Place in food processor with green onion mixture; pulse just until cod is coarsely chopped. Transfer cod mixture and 2 tablespoons panko to bowl with egg white; stir until well combined.

4   On large sheet of waxed paper, place remaining panko. With measuring cup, scoop out heaping ¼ cup cod mixture (mixture will be soft); shape by hand into 3" by 1½" stick (about 1 inch thick), then place in panko, patting gently to cover all sides. Place fish stick on prepared cookie sheet. Repeat, forming 8 fish sticks in all. Cover loosely; refrigerate at least 30 minutes and up to 1 day.

5   Into bowl with lime juice mixture, stir mayonnaise, sour cream, and remaining ⅛ teaspoon salt until well blended. If not using right away, cover and refrigerate up to 1 day. Makes about ⅓ cup sauce.

6   When ready to cook, preheat oven to 450°F. Lightly spray fish with cooking spray; bake 10 to 13 minutes or until opaque throughout. Cut remaining
lime into wedges. Arrange spinach on plates; top with fish and sauce. Serve
with lime wedges.

190 CALORIES   **PER SERVING.** 24G PROTEIN | 12G CARBOHYDRATE | 5G TOTAL FAT (1G SATURATED)
5G FIBER | 54MG CHOLESTEROL | 585MG SODIUM

MAKE IT A MEAL: **Kids and adults alike will enjoy these crispy fish sticks.
For a 350-calorie finger-food lunch, serve with Light Potato Salad (160 calories;
page 120).**

SPICY TURKEY JAMBALAYA

This hearty Creole classic gets slimmed down with chicken tenders and turkey sausage (in place of high-fat pork). Brown rice boosts the fiber and key phytonutrients, while peppers and tomatoes deliver half the daily recommendation of vitamin C . . . and it's all cooked in one skillet. For photo, see page 9.

ACTIVE TIME: 10 MINUTES · TOTAL TIME: 25 MINUTES

MAKES: 4 MAIN-DISH SERVINGS

---

8   OUNCES TURKEY ANDOUILLE
    SAUSAGE, SLICED ¼ INCH THICK

1   GREEN OR YELLOW PEPPER, CHOPPED

1   CAN (14½ OUNCES) STEWED
    TOMATOES

1   CUP UNCOOKED INSTANT
    BROWN RICE

8   OUNCES CHICKEN TENDERS, EACH
    CUT CROSSWISE IN HALF

½   CUP WATER

¼   TEASPOON SALT

1   BUNCH GREEN ONIONS, SLICED

1   Heat 12-inch skillet on medium until hot. Add sausage and pepper and cook 5 minutes, stirring occasionally.

2   Stir in tomatoes with their juice, rice, chicken, water, and salt; heat to boiling on high. Reduce heat to low; cover and simmer 10 minutes or until rice is just tender. Remove skillet from heat; stir in green onions.

265 CALORIES

PER SERVING. 26G PROTEIN | 30G CARBOHYDRATE | 6G TOTAL FAT (2G SATURATED) 4G FIBER | 73MG CHOLESTEROL | 830MG SODIUM

MAKE IT A MEAL: This spicy chicken and rice dish is a meal in a pan. For a sweet finale, add our creamy Chocolate Pudding (180 calories; page 149). The complete meal is just 445 calories.

BACON-WRAPPED SCALLOPS

In 30 minutes, this elegant-looking summer dish is ready for your family or friends to enjoy.

TOTAL TIME: 30 MINUTES
MAKES: 4 MAIN-DISH SERVINGS

4   EARS CORN, HUSKS AND SILKS REMOVED

4   SLICES BACON

16 LARGE SEA SCALLOPS

¼   TEASPOON BLACK PEPPER

2   MEDIUM TOMATOES (6 TO 8 OUNCES EACH), CHOPPED

2   RIPE NECTARINES, CHOPPED

¼   CUP CHOPPED FRESH BASIL LEAVES

2   TABLESPOONS LEMON JUICE

1   PINCH CAYENNE (GROUND RED) PEPPER

¼   TEASPOON SALT

1   Prepare outdoor grill for covered direct grilling over medium-high heat.

2   Grill corn 10 minutes or until browned, turning occasionally. Meanwhile, on microwave-safe plate, place bacon between paper towels. Microwave on High 1 minute.

3   Press 4 scallops together, flat sides down, in single layer; wrap with 1 slice bacon. Insert skewer through overlapping ends of bacon, pressing through to other side of scallops. Repeat with remaining scallops and bacon. Sprinkle black pepper on scallops.

4   Grill, covered, 5 to 7 minutes or until scallops are just opaque throughout, turning once.

5   Cut kernels off cobs and place in large bowl. Stir in tomatoes, nectarines, basil, lemon juice, cayenne, and salt. Serve with scallops.

215 CALORIES | **PER SERVING.** 16G PROTEIN | 30G CARBOHYDRATE | 5G TOTAL FAT (1G SATURATED) 4G FIBER | 25MG CHOLESTEROL | 290MG SODIUM ✅ ♥

MAKE IT A MEAL: Entertaining? Serve this for lunch or a light dinner with our Angel Food Cake (115 calories per serving; page 143) for dessert. Top each slice of cake with ½ cup raspberries (30 calories) for a heart-healthy 360-calorie meal.

HALIBUT WITH CORN SALSA

Mild and satisfyingly meaty, halibut gets instant oomph from a garden-ripe garnish of briny green olives, corn, and tomatoes.

ACTIVE TIME: 20 MINUTES · TOTAL TIME: 30 MINUTES
MAKES: 4 MAIN-DISH SERVINGS

4   SKINLESS HALIBUT OR COD FILLETS (6 OUNCES EACH)

1   PINCH CAYENNE (GROUND RED) PEPPER

½   TEASPOON SALT

1   POUND PLUM TOMATOES, CHOPPED

½   CUP PITTED GREEN OLIVES, THINLY SLICED

1   TABLESPOON CHAMPAGNE VINEGAR

1   TABLESPOON FRESH LEMON JUICE

2   TABLESPOONS EXTRA-VIRGIN OLIVE OIL

1   SMALL SHALLOT, FINELY CHOPPED

1½ CUPS FRESH CORN KERNELS

2   TABLESPOONS SNIPPED FRESH CHIVES, PLUS ADDITIONAL FOR GARNISH

1   TABLESPOON FINELY CHOPPED FRESH MINT LEAVES, PLUS ADDITIONAL FOR GARNISH

1   Fill 5-quart saucepot with *1 inch water*. Fit a steamer insert or basket into saucepot. (Water should not touch bottom of steamer.) Cover and heat to boiling, then reduce heat to low to maintain very gentle simmer.

2   Season both sides of fish with cayenne and ¼ teaspoon salt; place in single layer in steamer. Cover and steam 20 minutes or until opaque throughout.

3   Meanwhile, in large bowl, combine tomatoes, olives, vinegar, lemon juice, 1 tablespoon oil, and remaining ¼ teaspoon salt. Set tomato mixture aside.

4   In 12-inch skillet, heat remaining 1 tablespoon oil on medium-high. Add shallot and cook 1 minute or until browned, stirring. Add corn and cook 2 to 3 minutes or until browned, stirring occasionally. Transfer to bowl with tomato mixture. Add herbs and stir until well mixed.

5   Divide tomato mixture among serving plates. Remove steamer from saucepot. Carefully remove fish from steamer and place on top of tomato mixture on each plate. Garnish with chives and mint; serve immediately.

360 CALORIES   **PER SERVING.** 42G PROTEIN | 17G CARBOHYDRATE | 14G TOTAL FAT (2G SATURATED) 3G FIBER | 68MG CHOLESTEROL | 640MG SODIUM

MAKE IT A MEAL: Pair with a glass of crisp white wine (120 calories).

STEAK WITH OVEN FRIES

While the potatoes are in the oven, you can pan-fry the steak, make the red-wine-and-shallot sauce, and even whip up a salad and dressing.

ACTIVE TIME: 15 MINUTES · TOTAL TIME: 40 MINUTES

MAKES: 4 MAIN-DISH SERVINGS

OVEN FRIES (PAGE 118)

1   BEEF FLANK STEAK (1 POUND)

¼   TEASPOON COARSELY GROUND
    BLACK PEPPER

2   TEASPOONS OLIVE OIL

1   LARGE SHALLOT, FINELY CHOPPED

½   CUP DRY RED WINE

½   CUP CANNED CHICKEN BROTH

2   TABLESPOONS CHOPPED FRESH
    PARSLEY

1   Prepare Oven Fries.

2   Meanwhile, pat steak dry with paper towels; sprinkle on both sides with pepper. Heat nonstick 12-inch skillet over medium heat until hot. Add steak and cook 7 to 8 minutes per side, turning once, for medium-rare, or until desired doneness. (Instant-read thermometer inserted horizontally into center of steak should register 145°F.) Transfer steak to cutting board; keep warm.

3   To drippings in skillet, add oil; heat over medium heat. Add shallot and cook, stirring occasionally, until golden, about 2 minutes. Increase heat to medium-high. Add wine and broth; heat to boiling. Cook 3 to 4 minutes. Stir in parsley.

4   To serve, holding knife almost parallel to cutting surface, slice steak crosswise into thin slices. Spoon red-wine sauce over steak slices and serve with Oven Fries.

390
CALORIES

PER SERVING (WITH OVEN FRIES). 31G PROTEIN | 40G CARBOHYDRATE | 11G TOTAL FAT (4G SATURATED) | 3G FIBER | 46MG CHOLESTEROL | 455MG SODIUM ♥

MAKE IT A MEAL: This dish pairs nicely with a simple salad such as romaine tossed with a vinaigrette of your choice (120 calories). The steak, fries, and salad come to just over 500 calories per serving—amazing!

BORDER TOWN TACO SALAD

This Mexican taco salad is ready in just 30 minutes—and satisfying for either lunch or dinner.

TOTAL TIME: 30 MINUTES

MAKES: 4 MAIN-DISH SERVINGS

1 POUND (LEAN) GROUND BEEF OR GROUND CHICKEN

1½ TEASPOONS CHILI POWDER

¾ CUP PREPARED SALSA

10 OUNCES ROMAINE LETTUCE, CHOPPED

2 CUPS BAKED TORTILLA CHIPS

⅓ CUP REDUCED-FAT MEXICAN CHEESE BLEND, SHREDDED

1 MEDIUM AVOCADO, PITTED AND CUT INTO ½-INCH CHUNKS

2 TABLESPOONS REDUCED-FAT SOUR CREAM

1 In 12-inch skillet, cook ground beef on medium 4 to 5 minutes or until beef begins to brown, breaking up meat with spatula as it cooks. Stir in chili powder and cook 1 minute longer. Add ½ cup salsa and cook 3 to 4 minutes to heat through.

2 Meanwhile, divide lettuce among 4 serving plates. Top each with beef mixture, tortilla chips, cheese, avocado, sour cream, and remaining ¼ cup salsa.

385 CALORIES

PER SERVING. 28G PROTEIN | 20G CARBOHYDRATE | 22G TOTAL FAT (7G SATURATED) 6G FIBER | 84MG CHOLESTEROL | 635MG SODIUM

MAKE IT A MEAL: For an easy, 485-calorie dinner, finish with 1 cup fresh mango slices (100 calories).

LIGHTER BEEF AND BROCCOLI

Try our streamlined version of the popular Chinese dish—it's almost as quick as ordering takeout.

COOK TIME: 10 MINUTES · TOTAL TIME: 25 MINUTES
MAKES: 4 MAIN-DISH SERVINGS

1 LARGE BUNCH (1½ POUNDS) BROCCOLI
1 POUND BEEF TENDERLOIN STEAKS, TRIMMED AND CUT INTO ⅛-INCH-THICK STRIPS
3 GARLIC CLOVES, CRUSHED WITH GARLIC PRESS
1 TABLESPOON GRATED, PEELED FRESH GINGER
¼ TEASPOON CRUSHED RED PEPPER
1 TEASPOON OLIVE OIL
¾ CUP CANNED CHICKEN BROTH
3 TABLESPOONS SOY SAUCE
1 TABLESPOON CORNSTARCH
½ TEASPOON ASIAN SESAME OIL

1 From bunch, cut broccoli flowerets about 1½ inches long. Peel broccoli stems and cut into ¼-inch-thick diagonal slices.

2 In nonstick 12-inch skillet, heat ½ inch water to boiling over medium heat. Add broccoli and cook 3 to 4 minutes, uncovered, or until tender-crisp. Drain broccoli and set aside. Wipe skillet dry.

3 In medium bowl, toss beef with garlic, ginger, and crushed red pepper. Add ½ teaspoon olive oil to skillet and heat over medium heat until hot but not smoking. Add half of beef mixture and cook 3 minutes or until beef just loses its pink color throughout, stirring quickly and frequently. Transfer beef to plate. Repeat with remaining ½ teaspoon olive oil and beef mixture.

4 In cup, mix broth, soy sauce, cornstarch, and sesame oil until blended. Return cooked beef to skillet. Stir in cornstarch mixture; heat to boiling. Cook 1 minute or until sauce thickens slightly, stirring. Add broccoli and toss to coat.

245 CALORIES

PER SERVING. 28G PROTEIN | 10G CARBOHYDRATE | 11G TOTAL FAT (3G SATURATED) 3G FIBER | 57MG CHOLESTEROL | 1,010MG SODIUM ●

MAKE IT A MEAL: Add on 1 cup cooked white rice (205 calories) and a fortune cookie (30 calories). The complete meal is a guilt-free 480 calories.

SMOTHERED PORK CHOPS

Pan-fried pork chops are smothered in a fragrant, mushroom-filled gravy and served with a side of green beans. For photo, see page 36.

ACTIVE TIME: 20 MINUTES · **TOTAL TIME:** 50 MINUTES
MAKES: 4 MAIN-DISH SERVINGS

3 TABLESPOONS PLUS 1 TEASPOON WHITE WHOLE-WHEAT OR ALL-PURPOSE FLOUR

½ TEASPOON SALT

½ TEASPOON GROUND BLACK PEPPER

4 (¾-INCH-THICK) BONELESS CENTER-CUT PORK CHOPS (5 OUNCES EACH)

1 TABLESPOON CANOLA OIL

2 LARGE ONIONS (12 OUNCES EACH), THINLY SLICED

3 GARLIC CLOVES, CHOPPED

2 CONTAINERS (8 OUNCES EACH) CREMINI MUSHROOMS, SLICED

½ TEASPOON DRIED ROSEMARY

1 CUP CANNED REDUCED-SODIUM CHICKEN BROTH

1 BAG (12 OUNCES) MICROWAVE-IN-THE-BAG GREEN BEANS

1 Sprinkle 1 teaspoon flour and ¼ teaspoon each salt and pepper all over chops. In 12-inch skillet, heat oil on medium-high. Cook pork 7 minutes or until browned, turning over once. Transfer to plate.

2 To same skillet, add onions and garlic. Reduce heat to medium; cook 5 minutes or until browned, stirring frequently. Add mushrooms and rosemary; cook 6 to 8 minutes or until mushrooms are tender, stirring occasionally. Add 3 tablespoons flour; cook 3 minutes, stirring constantly.

3 Add broth in slow, steady stream, stirring constantly. Heat to simmering and return pork to pan in single layer; spoon onion mixture on top. Cover, reduce heat, and simmer 8 minutes or until pork is barely pink in center; instant-read thermometer inserted horizontally into thickest part of pork chop should register 145°F. Stir in remaining ¼ teaspoon each salt and pepper.

4 While pork simmers, microwave green beans as label directs. Arrange beans on plates with pork and sauce.

395 CALORIES

PER SERVING. 34G PROTEIN | 30G CARBOHYDRATE | 18G TOTAL FAT (6G SATURATED) 6G FIBER | 74MG CHOLESTEROL | 955MG SODIUM 🌱

MAKE IT A MEAL: After you've finished preparing this dinner, sit back and enjoy it with a glass of red wine (120 calories).

PORK LOIN WITH PEACH GLAZE

Pork tenderloin is as lean as skinless chicken breast, with only 3 grams of fat and 120 calories per 3-ounce serving. Grill it with fresh peaches to add health-boosting fiber, carbs, and vitamins A and C.

ACTIVE TIME: 10 MINUTES · TOTAL TIME: 20 MINUTES
MAKES: 4 MAIN-DISH SERVINGS

1	LIME	2	BUNCHES GREEN ONIONS
½	CUP PEACH PRESERVES	1	TEASPOON OLIVE OIL
¾	TEASPOON SALT	4	MEDIUM PEACHES, EACH CUT IN HALF AND PITTED
⅜	TEASPOON GROUND BLACK PEPPER		
1	PORK TENDERLOIN (1¼ POUNDS)		

1   Prepare outdoor grill for covered direct grilling over medium heat. From lime, grate 1 teaspoon peel and squeeze 1 tablespoon juice.

2   In medium bowl, combine preserves, lime peel and juice, ½ teaspoon salt, and ¼ teaspoon pepper. Reserve ¼ cup glaze in small bowl.

3   Cut pork tenderloin crosswise in half, then cut each piece lengthwise in half. Place pork on hot grill rack; cover and cook 5 minutes. Turn pork over; brush with glaze from medium bowl. Cover and cook 5 to 6 minutes longer or until pork is browned outside and still slightly pink inside, brushing several times with glaze. (Instant-read thermometer inserted horizontally into thickest part of pork should register 145°F.) Transfer to cutting board.

4   Meanwhile, toss green onions with oil and remaining ¼ teaspoon salt and ⅛ teaspoon pepper. Place onions and peaches, cut sides down, on same grill rack; cook 3 minutes, turning onions over once. Transfer onions to platter. Turn peaches over and brush with glaze from small bowl; cook 3 minutes longer or until browned. Transfer to platter with green onions.

5   Slice pork and serve with peaches and green onions.

330 CALORIES

PER SERVING. 32G PROTEIN | 43G CARBOHYDRATE | 5G TOTAL FAT (2G SATURATED) 4G FIBER | 78MG CHOLESTEROL | 515MG SODIUM ◔

> MAKE IT A MEAL: Serve this luscious main with 1 cup steamed asparagus (40 calories). For dessert, crunch on a Pecan Finger (120 calories; page 145). Total calories for this supper: just 490.

400
CALORIES

*Spanish Chicken
and Rice
(page 60)*

COZY CASSEROLES

Mac and cheese, chicken potpie, and lasagna—nothing says comfort like these old-fashioned favorites. Unfortunately, an overdose of calories and fat often come hand in hand with the comfort. Not so with our 400 calorie or less casseroles. Through creative substitutions, we've cut the calories and fat without sacrificing the flavor and ooey-gooey goodness of these dishes. Reduced-fat cheese and milk stand in for the full-fat versions, while ground turkey and turkey sausage deliver leaner casseroles than beef or pork. Plus, ample doses of whole grains and plenty of fresh vegetables ramp up the nutritional value of these one-dish wonders.

KEY TO ICONS

30 minutes or less   Heart healthy   High fiber   Make ahead   Slow cooker

BROCCOLI MAC AND CHEESE

A classic mac and cheese is made healthier—and more colorful—with broccoli florets and a sprinkling of whole-wheat breadcrumbs.

ACTIVE TIME: 26 MINUTES · TOTAL TIME: 40 MINUTES
MAKES: 8 MAIN-DISH SERVINGS

2	SLICES WHOLE-WHEAT BREAD	1	BOX (16 OUNCES) ELBOW MACARONI
8	OUNCES REDUCED-FAT EXTRA-SHARP CHEDDAR CHEESE, SHREDDED (2¼ CUPS)	¼	TEASPOON SALT
		½	TEASPOON FRESHLY GROUND PEPPER
2	TABLESPOONS CORNSTARCH	1	POUND SMALL BROCCOLI FLORETS
3¼	CUP LOW-FAT MILK (1%)	⅛	TEASPOON FRESHLY GRATED NUTMEG
6	OUNCES GOUDA CHEESE, SHREDDED (2 CUPS)		

1 Heat covered 8-quart saucepot with 6 quarts water to boiling on high.

2 Arrange oven rack 6 inches from broiler heat source. Preheat broiler. Tear bread into large chunks. In food processor with knife blade attached, pulse bread until crumbs form. In small bowl, combine breadcrumbs and ½ cup shredded Cheddar.

3 Meanwhile, in 3½- to 4-quart saucepot, whisk together cornstarch and ¼ cup milk. Heat on medium-high, gradually adding remaining 3 cups milk in a slow, steady stream, whisking constantly. Heat to boiling, whisking frequently, then cook 2 minutes longer, whisking constantly. Remove saucepot from heat and add Gouda and remaining Cheddar, stirring until cheeses are melted and sauce is smooth.

4 Add macaroni and 1 teaspoon salt to boiling water. Cook 1 minutes, stirring occasionally, then add the broccoli. Cook 4 to 5 minutes longer or until pasta is just tender but firm and broccoli is bright green and crisp-tender, stirring occasionally. Drain well, then immediately return to saucepot. Add sauce, nutmeg, remaining ¼ teaspoon salt, and ½ teaspoon pepper, stir over medium-low heat until well mixed.

5 Transfer mixture to 3-quart shallow baking dish. Sprinkle breadcrumb mixture evenly over top. Broil 1 to 2 minutes or until topping is golden brown.

400 CALORIES **PER SERVING.** 22G PROTEIN | 57G CARBOHYDRATE | 11G TOTAL FAT (6G SATURATED) 5G FIBER | 36MG CHOLESTEROL | 490MG SODIUM 🌱 🍽

MAKE IT A MEAL: Serve with a salad of halved cherry tomatoes tossed with light balsamic vinaigrette for a less-than-500-calorie dinner.

LASAGNA ROLLS

A pan of hot, bubbly lasagna has timeless appeal.

ACTIVE TIME: 25 MINUTES · TOTAL TIME: 1 HOUR 10 MINUTES
MAKES: 6 MAIN-DISH SERVINGS

8 OUNCES CURLY LASAGNA NOODLES

2 CANS (14½ OUNCES EACH) STEWED TOMATOES

1 CAN (8 OUNCES) TOMATO SAUCE

1 CONTAINER (15 OUNCES) PART-SKIM RICOTTA CHEESE

6 OUNCES PART-SKIM MOZZARELLA CHEESE, SHREDDED (1½ CUPS)

3 TABLESPOONS FRESHLY GRATED PARMESAN CHEESE

½ TEASPOON COARSELY GROUND BLACK PEPPER

4 TABLESPOONS CHOPPED FRESH BASIL

2 TEASPOONS OLIVE OIL

1 SMALL ONION, CHOPPED

1 SMALL ZUCCHINI (6 OUNCES), DICED

1 SMALL RIPE TOMATO (4 OUNCES), DICED

1 TABLESPOON CAPERS, DRAINED AND CHOPPED

1 Prepare lasagna noodles as label directs. Drain and rinse with cold running water to stop cooking. Return noodles to pot with cold water to cover.
2 Meanwhile, in 3-quart glass or ceramic baking dish, combine stewed tomatoes with their juice and tomato sauce, breaking up tomatoes with side of spoon. In large bowl, mix ricotta, mozzarella, Parmesan, pepper, and 3 tablespoons basil. Preheat oven to 375°F.
4 Drain lasagna noodles on clean kitchen towels. Spread rounded ¼ cup cheese filling over each lasagna noodle and roll up jelly-roll fashion. Slice each rolled noodle crosswise in half. Arrange lasagna rolls, cut sides down, in sauce in baking dish; cover loosely with foil. Bake until hot, 35 to 40 minutes.
5 Meanwhile, prepare topping: In nonstick 10-inch skillet, heat oil over medium heat. Add onion and cook until tender and browned. Add zucchini and cook until tender. Stir in diced tomato, capers, and remaining 1 tablespoon basil; heat through.
6 To serve, place tomato sauce and lasagna rolls on plates and spoon zucchini topping over lasagna rolls.

385 CALORIES

PER SERVING. 24G PROTEIN | 43G CARBOHYDRATE | 14G TOTAL FAT (7G SATURATED)
4G FIBER | 40MG CHOLESTEROL | 910MG SODIUM

MAKE IT A MEAL: For a 480-calorie Italian-style meal, add on a slice of toasted Italian bread dipped in 1 teaspoon extra-virgin olive oil (95 calories). *Mangia!*

CHICKEN POTPIE

Loaded with white-meat chicken and lots of hearty root vegetables, this healthy potpie makes the perfect family meal.

ACTIVE TIME: 30 MINUTES · **TOTAL TIME:** 1 HOUR
MAKES: 6 MAIN-DISH SERVINGS

¼ TEASPOON DRIED THYME

¾ TEASPOON SALT

½ TEASPOON GROUND BLACK PEPPER

1½ POUNDS SKINLESS, BONELESS CHICKEN BREASTS, CUT INTO 1-INCH CHUNKS

OLIVE OIL COOKING SPRAY

1 LARGE ONION (12 OUNCES), FINELY CHOPPED

1 CAN (14½ OUNCES) REDUCED-SODIUM CHICKEN BROTH

2 GARLIC CLOVES, CHOPPED

1 POUND PARSNIPS, PEELED AND THINLY SLICED

3 CARROTS, THINLY SLICED

3 STALKS CELERY, THINLY SLICED

6 SHEETS FROZEN PHYLLO (EACH 14" BY 9"), THAWED

2 TABLESPOONS CORNSTARCH

½ CUP WATER

2 CUPS FROZEN PEAS, THAWED

¼ CUP FINELY CHOPPED FRESH FLAT-LEAF PARSLEY

1 Preheat oven to 425°F.

2 Sprinkle thyme and ¼ teaspoon each salt and pepper evenly over chicken. Lightly coat 12-inch skillet with olive oil spray; heat on medium-high. Add chicken in single layer and cook 3 minutes or until lightly browned, turning pieces over once halfway through cooking; transfer to plate.

3 To same skillet, add onion and ¼ cup chicken broth. Cook 5 minutes or until browned, stirring and scraping up browned bits from bottom of pan. Add garlic and cook 1 minute, stirring. Stir in parsnips, carrots, and celery, then add remaining 1½ cups chicken broth. Heat to boiling on high. Cover, and reduce heat to maintain simmer. Cook 10 minutes or until vegetables are tender-crisp.

4 While vegetables cook, place 1 phyllo sheet on work surface; spray lightly with olive oil spray. Top with another sheet. Repeat with remaining phyllo sheets and olive oil spray, lightly coating top sheet with spray.

5 In small bowl, stir cornstarch into water to dissolve; stir into vegetable mixture and simmer 2 minutes or until thickened, stirring occasionally. Stir in peas, chopped parsley, reserved chicken, and remaining ½ teaspoon salt and ¼ teaspoon pepper. Heat to simmering, then transfer to 13" by 9" by 2" baking dish. Center phyllo on top, tucking in edges if necessary; cut five slits in phyllo.

6   Bake 15 minutes or until phyllo is golden brown. To serve, use a serrated knife to slice through pastry, then scoop into bowls.

330 CALORIES   **PER SERVING.** 30G PROTEIN | 41G CARBOHYDRATE | 5G TOTAL FAT (1G SATURATED)
8G FIBER | 73MG CHOLESTEROL | 705MG SODIUM 🌱

MAKE IT A MEAL: Tin Roof Treats (135 calories; page 146) are the perfect finish to this nostalgic meal. You can enjoy it all for just 465 calories.

SPANISH CHICKEN AND RICE

Chicken and rice gets a Spanish twist from peppers, olives, and a healthy dose of sweet, smoky paprika. For photo, see page 54.

ACTIVE TIME: 35 MINUTES · TOTAL TIME: 1 HOUR

MAKES: 4 MAIN-DISH SERVINGS

1½ TEASPOONS OLIVE OIL

4 SKINLESS, BONE-IN CHICKEN THIGHS

¼ TEASPOON SALT

⅛ TEASPOON COARSELY GROUND BLACK PEPPER

1 GREEN PEPPER, CUT INTO ½-INCH PIECES

1 GARLIC CLOVE, CRUSHED WITH PRESS

1 SMALL ONION (6 OUNCES), CHOPPED

1½ TEASPOONS PAPRIKA

1 CAN (14½ OUNCES EACH) DICED TOMATOES IN JUICE

¾ CUP CHICKEN BROTH

1½ CUPS WATER

1¼ CUPS LONG-GRAIN WHITE RICE

1 CUP FROZEN PEAS

½ CUP SALAD OLIVES OR COARSELY CHOPPED PIMIENTO-STUFFED OLIVES

1 Preheat oven to 350°F. In 5- to 6-quart Dutch oven, heat oil on medium-high until hot. Sprinkle chicken all over with salt and black pepper; cook about 6 minutes per batch, until lightly browned on both sides. With tongs, transfer chicken pieces to small roasting pan (13" by 9").

2 Cover roasting pan with foil and bake chicken 25 to 30 minutes, until instant-read thermometer inserted in thickest part of thigh registers 165°F.

3 Meanwhile, in same Dutch oven, cook green pepper, garlic, and onion about 10 minutes or until vegetables are tender, stirring occasionally. Stir in paprika and cook 30 seconds. Add tomatoes with their juice, broth, water, and rice; heat to boiling on high. Reduce heat to low; cover and simmer 10 minutes. Stir in frozen peas and olives.

4 Grease 2½-quart ceramic baking dish. Spoon rice mixture into prepared baking dish; tuck thighs into hot rice mixture. Cover and bake 25 minutes or until rice is tender and most of liquid is absorbed. Fluff rice to serve.

400 CALORIES

PER SERVING. 21G PROTEIN | 56G CARBOHYDRATE | 9G TOTAL FAT (2G SATURATED) 5G FIBER | 49MG CHOLESTEROL | 754MG SODIUM 🌱 🍴

MAKE IT A MEAL: Enjoy this one-dish dinner with a glass of Spanish wine (520 calories for the meal).

TURKEY LEFTOVERS PIE

Wondering what to do with turkey and mashed potato leftovers? Make a pie! Your leftover mashed potatoes will be cold and stiff, but all you have to do is add a few tablespoons of hot milk and stir them and they'll become loose enough to spread.

ACTIVE TIME: 10 MINUTES · TOTAL TIME: 35 MINUTES PLUS STANDING

MAKES: 6 MAIN-DISH SERVINGS

4	TABLESPOONS BUTTER OR MARGARINE	2	CUPS LEFTOVER COOKED VEGETABLES, COARSELY CHOPPED
2	TABLESPOONS ALL-PURPOSE FLOUR	½	CUP LEFTOVER STUFFING
1	CAN (14½ OUNCES) CHICKEN BROTH	2	CUPS LEFTOVER MASHED POTATOES
1	TEASPOON WORCESTERSHIRE SAUCE	2	OUNCES SHARP CHEDDAR CHEESE, SHREDDED (½ CUP)
2	CUPS LEFTOVER COOKED TURKEY, CUT INTO ½-INCH PIECES		

1 Preheat oven to 375°F. Lightly grease shallow 2-quart glass or ceramic baking dish; set aside.

2 In 3-quart saucepan, melt butter on medium. Whisk in flour until smooth; cook 1 minute. Whisk in broth and Worcestershire sauce until well blended; heat to boiling on high. Reduce heat to low and simmer 5 minutes, stirring frequently. Stir in turkey and chopped vegetables. Spoon stuffing evenly into bottom of prepared baking dish. Top with turkey mixture. Using back of spoon, evenly spread mashed potatoes over top; sprinkle with shredded cheese.

3 Bake 25 minutes or until casserole is hot and bubbly and cheese begins to brown at edges. Let stand 5 minutes for easier serving.

340 CALORIES

PER SERVING. 22G PROTEIN | 33G CARBOHYDRATE | 14G TOTAL FAT (4G SATURATED) 4G FIBER | 47MG CHOLESTEROL | 830MG SODIUM

MAKE IT A MEAL: For dessert, try our chocolate-chip-studded Cocoa Brownies (120 calories; page 144) for a 460-calorie dinner.

POLENTA AND CHILI POTPIE

Polenta is the ultimate quick-dinner trick. Cornmeal simmered—in the microwave!—in a mixture of water and low-fat milk becomes a creamy crust for a fun and tasty chili potpie.

ACTIVE TIME: 30 MINUTES · TOTAL TIME: 2 HOURS 20 MINUTES PLUS STANDING
MAKES: 10 MAIN-DISH SERVINGS

CHILI

2   TEASPOONS OLIVE OIL

1½ POUNDS WELL-TRIMMED BONELESS BEEF CHUCK, CUT INTO ½-INCH PIECES

¾   TEASPOON SALT

1   ONION, CHOPPED

1   RED PEPPER, CHOPPED

3   GARLIC CLOVES, CRUSHED WITH GARLIC PRESS

1   SERRANO OR JALAPEÑO CHILE, SEEDED AND FINELY CHOPPED

2   TABLESPOONS TOMATO PASTE

3   TABLESPOONS CHILI POWDER

1   TABLESPOON GROUND CUMIN

1   CAN (28 OUNCES) WHOLE TOMATOES IN JUICE

2   CANS (15 TO 19 OUNCES EACH) RED KIDNEY BEANS, RINSED AND DRAINED

POLENTA CRUST

2   CUPS LOW-FAT MILK (1%)

1½ CUPS CORNMEAL

¾   TEASPOON SALT

4½ CUPS BOILING WATER

1   Prepare chili: In 12-inch skillet with broiler-safe handle, heat oil over medium-high heat until hot. Sprinkle beef with ¼ teaspoon salt.
2   Add beef to skillet in 2 batches and cook 4 to 5 minutes per batch or until beef is browned on all sides, stirring occasionally and adding more oil if necessary. With slotted spoon, transfer beef to bowl when it is browned.
3   After all beef is browned, add onion, red pepper, garlic, and serrano to same skillet and cook over medium heat, stirring occasionally, until all vegetables are lightly browned and tender, about 8 minutes. Stir in tomato paste, chili powder, cumin, and remaining ½ teaspoon salt; cook 1 minute, stirring constantly.
4   Return beef and any juices in bowl to skillet. Add tomatoes with their juice, stirring and breaking up tomatoes with side of spoon; heat to boiling over medium-high heat.
5   Reduce heat to low; cover and simmer 1 hour and 15 minutes, stirring occasionally. Add beans and cook, uncovered, 15 minutes longer or until meat is tender.
6   Meanwhile, prepare polenta crust: After adding beans to chili, in micro-wave-safe deep 4-quart bowl or casserole, combine milk, cornmeal, and salt until blended; whisk in boiling water.

7 Cook in microwave on High 12 to 15 minutes. After first 5 minutes of cooking, whisk vigorously until smooth (mixture will be lumpy at first). Stir twice more during cooking. While polenta is cooking, preheat broiler.

8 When chili is done, skim off and discard fat. Spread polenta evenly over chili in skillet. Place skillet in broiler 6 to 8 inches from source of heat and broil 3 to 4 minutes or until polenta crust is lightly browned, rotating skillet if necessary for even browning. Let pie stand 10 minutes for easier serving.

325 CALORIES **PER SERVING.** 26G PROTEIN | 44G CARBOHYDRATE | 7G TOTAL FAT (2G SATURATED) 11G FIBER | 34MG CHOLESTEROL | 780MG SODIUM 🌱

MAKE IT A MEAL: Serve with Corn and Avocado Salad (180 calories; page 134) for a satisfying dinner that's just over 500 calories.

NACHO CASSEROLE

This cheesy Mexican-inspired casserole is fun food to enjoy on movie night or while watching the big game. To put a cap on the calories, fat, and sodium, we swapped in baked, unsalted tortilla chips, fat-free refried beans, and used low-fat milk for added creaminess. For less heat, cut down on or omit the jalapeños.

TOTAL TIME: 30 MINUTES

MAKES: 6 MAIN-DISH SERVINGS

1   CAN (10¾ OUNCES) CHEDDAR CHEESE SOUP

½   CUP LOW-FAT MILK (1%)

1   JAR (16 OUNCES) MILD OR MEDIUM-HOT SALSA

1   BAG (7 OUNCES) BAKED, UNSALTED TORTILLA CHIPS

1   CAN (16 OUNCES) FAT-FREE REFRIED BEANS

2   JALAPEÑO CHILES, THINLY SLICED

1   CUP SHREDDED CHEDDAR CHEESE

1   Preheat oven to 400°F. In 13" by 9" ceramic or glass baking dish, stir undiluted soup with milk; spread evenly. Top with half of salsa and half of chips. Carefully spread beans over chips. Top with remaining chips and salsa. Sprinkle with jalapeños and Cheddar.

2   Bake 20 minutes or until hot.

385 CALORIES

PER SERVING. 17G PROTEIN | 60G CARBOHYDRATE | 12G TOTAL FAT (5G SATURATED) 5G FIBER | 27MG CHOLESTEROL | 1,370MG SODIUM ✔ ✿

MAKE IT A MEAL: To create a 450-calorie supper, serve with 2 cups mixed greens topped with ¼ cup ripe avocado cubes (65 calories).

BEEF TAMALE PIE

A terrific, family-friendly recipe.

TOTAL TIME: 25 MINUTES

MAKES: 4 MAIN-DISH SERVINGS

1 LOG (16 OUNCES) PRECOOKED POLENTA, CUT CROSSWISE INTO 8 SLICES

1 PACKAGE (17 OUNCES) FULLY COOKED ROAST BEEF AU JUS

1 CAN (14½ OUNCES) DICED TOMATOES WITH GREEN CHILES

2 TEASPOONS CHILI POWDER

½ CUP LOOSELY PACKED FRESH CILANTRO LEAVES

1 CUP FROZEN CORN KERNELS

4 OUNCES SHREDDED MEXICAN CHEESE BLEND (1 CUP)

1 Preheat broiler and position rack as close as possible to heat source. Place polenta slices on cookie sheet and broil 10 to 12 minutes or until polenta is golden on top.

2 Meanwhile, drain beef jus into 12-inch skillet. Add tomatoes with their juice and chili powder; heat to boiling over high heat. Boil 4 to 5 minutes or until sauce thickens. While mixture boils, shred beef with two forks. Coarsely chop cilantro.

3 Stir frozen corn and beef into tomato mixture; heat through. Remove saucepan from heat; stir in all but 1 teaspoon cilantro. Arrange polenta over beef mixture; sprinkle with cheese and remaining cilantro. Cover skillet; let stand 2 minutes or until cheese melts.

380 CALORIES

PER SERVING. 30G PROTEIN | 34G CARBOHYDRATE | 14G TOTAL FAT (8G SATURATED) 3G FIBER | 97MG CHOLESTEROL | 1,800MG SODIUM ◔

MAKE IT A MEAL: To add something fresh and colorful, serve with a side of Carrot and Zucchini Ribbons (40 calories; page 126) for a 420-calorie dinner.

SWEET POTATO SHEPHERD'S PIE

Shepherd's pie Louisiana style—with collard greens, sweet potatoes, and Cajun spices.

ACTIVE TIME: 30 MINUTES · **TOTAL TIME:** 1 HOUR 10 MINUTES
MAKES: 6 MAIN-DISH SERVINGS

2½ POUNDS SWEET POTATOES, WASHED

½ CUP WATER

½ CUP LOW-FAT MILK (1%)

½ TEASPOON SALT

¼ TEASPOON GROUND BLACK PEPPER

1 TABLESPOON PLUS 1 TEASPOON CANOLA OIL

1 LARGE ONION (12 OUNCES), FINELY CHOPPED

1 BUNCH (12 OUNCES) COLLARD GREENS, STEMS DISCARDED, LEAVES VERY THINLY SLICED

2 GARLIC CLOVES, CHOPPED

1 POUND LEAN GROUND TURKEY (93%)

2 TEASPOONS SALT-FREE CAJUN SEASONING

2 TABLESPOONS TOMATO PASTE

1 TABLESPOON FINELY CHOPPED FRESH FLAT-LEAF PARSLEY LEAVES, FOR GARNISH

1 Preheat oven to 400°F.

2 In large microwave-safe bowl, combine sweet potatoes and ¼ cup water. Cover with vented plastic wrap and microwave on High 15 minutes or until tender. When cool enough to handle, discard peels. In large bowl, mash potatoes with milk and ⅛ teaspoon each salt and pepper.

3 Meanwhile, in 12-inch skillet, heat 1 tablespoon oil on medium-high. Add onion and cook 5 minutes or until browned, stirring occasionally. Add collard greens and ⅛ teaspoon each salt and pepper. Cook 1 minute or until just wilted, stirring. Transfer to medium bowl.

4 In same skillet, heat remaining 1 teaspoon oil. Add garlic and cook 15 seconds. Add turkey and remaining ¼ teaspoon salt. Cook 3 minutes or until browned, breaking meat into small pieces and stirring. Reduce heat to medium and add Cajun seasoning. Cook 1 minute, stirring. Add tomato paste and remaining ¼ cup water. Cook 2 minutes, stirring.

5 In 8-inch square shallow baking dish, spread half of mashed sweet potatoes. Top with turkey mixture, then collard greens mixture. Spread remaining sweet potato mixture on top. Bake 30 minutes or until golden on top. Garnish with parsley.

290 CALORIES **PER SERVING.** 19G PROTEIN | 36G CARBOHYDRATE | 9G TOTAL FAT (2G SATURATED) 7G FIBER | 44MG CHOLESTEROL | 350MG SODIUM ♥ ◉ 🍴

MAKE IT A MEAL: Cook up Corn on the Cob with Spicy Butter (130 calories; page 132) for a down-home 420-calorie dinner.

SAUSAGE AND POLENTA

Traditional Italian polenta can be served in a variety of ways. Here, the recipe is spiced up with lean turkey sausage and ready to serve in a mere 30 minutes!

TOTAL TIME: 30 MINUTES

MAKES: 4 MAIN-DISH SERVINGS

1 LOG (16 OUNCES) PLAIN PRECOOKED POLENTA, CUT INTO 8 ROUNDS

2 TABLESPOONS GRATED PECORINO-ROMANO CHEESE

12 OUNCES ITALIAN TURKEY SAUSAGE, CASINGS REMOVED

2 MEDIUM ZUCCHINI (8 OUNCES EACH), CUT INTO 1-INCH CHUNKS

1 YELLOW PEPPER, CUT INTO 1-INCH CHUNKS

1 CUP PREPARED MARINARA SAUCE

¼ CUP WATER

1 Preheat broiler and position rack 5 to 6 inches from heat source. Line cookie sheet with foil sprayed with nonstick cooking spray. Place polenta on prepared sheet; broil 10 minutes or until golden, without turning over. Sprinkle polenta with Pecorino; broil 1 minute or until cheese melts.

2 Meanwhile, spray nonstick 12-inch skillet with nonstick spray; heat on medium until hot. Add sausage; cook 8 minutes or until browned, breaking up sausage with side of spoon. Add zucchini and yellow pepper; cook 3 minutes or until vegetables are tender-crisp, stirring often. Add marinara and water; simmer, covered, 8 minutes.

3 Place 2 polenta rounds on each plate; top with sausage sauce.

300 **PER SERVING.** 21G PROTEIN | 28G CARBOHYDRATE | 11G TOTAL FAT (3G SATURATED)
CALORIES 4G FIBER | 53MG CHOLESTEROL | 1,100MG SODIUM

MAKE IT A MEAL: For a simple 420-calorie meal, add on three cheese straws (120 calories) for crunch.

CHORIZO AND PEPPER TORTILLA

A traditional Spanish dish, a tortilla is a thick omelet composed of potato, onions, and egg. Our version also features spicy chorizo sausage and sautéed red peppers.

ACTIVE TIME: 25 MINUTES · TOTAL TIME: 50 MINUTES
MAKES: 6 MAIN-DISH SERVINGS

1   POUND SMALL RED POTATOES, THINLY SLICED

1   TEASPOON SALT

2   TABLESPOONS OLIVE OIL

1   MEDIUM ONION, THINLY SLICED

1   RED PEPPER, THINLY SLICED

1   GARLIC CLOVE, CRUSHED WITH PRESS

8   LARGE EGGS

1   PACKAGE (3½ OUNCES) FULLY COOKED CHORIZO SAUSAGE, CUT INTO ¼-INCH PIECES

¼   CUP LOOSELY PACKED FRESH PARSLEY LEAVES, CHOPPED

1   In 2-quart saucepan, place potatoes with enough *water* to cover and salt; heat to boiling on high. Reduce heat to low and simmer 3 to 5 minutes or until tender when pierced with knife. Drain potatoes; return to pan.

2   Meanwhile, preheat oven to 350°F. In nonstick 10-inch skillet with oven-safe handle, heat 1 tablespoon oil on medium 1 minute. Add onion, red pepper, and garlic; cook 12 minutes or until vegetables are tender and golden, stirring occasionally.

3   In large bowl, with fork, mix eggs, chorizo, and parsley until well blended. Gently stir in potatoes and onion mixture.

4   In same skillet, heat remaining 1 tablespoon oil on medium. Pour in egg mixture and place in oven. Bake 22 to 24 minutes or until knife inserted in center comes out clean and top is browned. Remove from oven.

5   Center large round plate upside down on top of skillet. Wearing oven mitts to protect your hands, and grasping plate and skillet firmly together, quickly invert tortilla onto plate. Slide onto cutting board to serve.

295 CALORIES

PER SERVING. 14G PROTEIN | 20G CARBOHYDRATE | 18G TOTAL FAT (5G SATURATED) 2G FIBER | 298MG CHOLESTEROL | 390MG SODIUM

MAKE IT A MEAL: For a 405-calorie brunch, serve with 2 cups mixed greens tossed with 100 calories of balsamic dressing (110 calories).

STUFFED PEPPERS

For a healthier take on this retro casserole, we stuffed a colorful mix of bell peppers with lean ground beef, whole grains, spinach, and crushed tomatoes and topped them off with a sprinkle of feta cheese and fresh dill.

ACTIVE TIME: 40 MINUTES · TOTAL TIME: 1 HOUR 15 MINUTES
MAKES: 4 MAIN-DISH SERVINGS

4 LARGE RED, YELLOW, ORANGE, AND/OR GREEN PEPPERS, WITH STEMS, IF POSSIBLE	1 PACKAGE (5 OUNCES) FROZEN CHOPPED SPINACH, THAWED AND SQUEEZED DRY
1 CAN (14½ OUNCES) CHICKEN BROTH	¼ CUP LOOSELY PACKED FRESH DILL, CHOPPED
¾ CUPS BULGUR	
½ TABLESPOON OLIVE OIL	1 CAN (28 OUNCES) CRUSHED TOMATOES
½ ONION, CHOPPED	2 OUNCES FETA CHEESE, CRUMBLED (½ CUP)
2 SMALL GARLIC CLOVES, CRUSHED WITH GARLIC PRESS	⅛ TEASPOON SALT
8 OUNCES LEAN GROUND BEEF (90%)	⅛ TEASPOON COARSELY GROUND BLACK PEPPER

1 Cut ¾-inch-thick slices from top of each pepper; reserve tops, including stems. Remove seeds and ribs, and cut thin slice from bottoms so peppers will stand upright.

2 Arrange peppers and tops (separately) on same microwave-safe plate. Cook, uncovered, in microwave on High 4 minutes. With tongs, transfer tops to paper towel. Microwave peppers 4 to 5 minutes longer, until just tender. Invert peppers onto double thickness of paper towels to drain.

3 In microwave-safe large bowl, combine broth and bulgur. Cook, uncovered, in microwave on High 12 to 15 minutes, until bulgur is tender but still slightly chewy and most of broth is absorbed.

4 Meanwhile, in deep 12-inch skillet, heat oil over medium heat until hot. Add onion and garlic and cook until onion begins to turn golden, about 5 minutes, stirring frequently. Remove 2 tablespoons onion mixture and reserve. Add beef to remaining onion in skillet and cook until beef is no longer pink, 6 to 8 minutes, breaking up beef with side of spoon. Remove skillet from heat.

5 Into beef in skillet, stir bulgur, spinach, dill, ½ cup crushed tomatoes, and 6 tablespoons feta. Fill peppers with bulgur mixture, using 1 generous cup for each; sprinkle with remaining 2 tablespoons feta. Replace pepper tops.

6 Preheat oven to 350°F. Wipe skillet clean.

7   In same skillet, combine remaining tomatoes, reserved onion mixture, salt, and pepper; heat to boiling over medium-high heat, stirring occasionally. Spread tomato in 2-quart shallow casserole or 8-inch square glass baking dish. Place peppers in dish, cover with foil, and bake until peppers are hot, about 35 minutes.

365
CALORIES

PER SERVING. 24G PROTEIN | 45G CARBOHYDRATE | 12G TOTAL FAT (5G SATURATED) 12G FIBER | 49MG CHOLESTEROL | 1,220MG SODIUM

MAKE IT A MEAL: For a complete 465-calorie dinner, serve with a wedge of our caramelized Maple Squash (100 calories; page 132).

345
CALORIES
Soy-Honey Pork Loin
(page 88)

SUCCULENT ROASTS

For family dinners and special celebrations, nothing beats a roast. Enjoy classics like our Roasted Lemon Chicken, Turkey Breast with Vegetable Gravy, Roast Beef with Horseradish Cream, and Mustard-Glazed Fresh Ham. Or surprise family and friends with our creative takes on the theme, such as Cod with Mushroom Ragout, Soy-Honey Pork Loin, and Glazed Meat Loaf, which supplements ground beef with turkey and oats to make a leaner loaf. All are as comforting as can be—and 400 calories or less per serving!

KEY TO ICONS

🕐 30 minutes or less   ♥ Heart healthy   🌾 High fiber   ▥ Make ahead   ▥ Slow cooker

HONEY-MUSTARD CHICKEN

Everything for this meal cooks in the oven at the same time—the red potatoes, onion, and the chicken breasts.

ACTIVE TIME: 10 MINUTES · TOTAL TIME: 1 HOUR 35 MINUTES
MAKES: 4 MAIN-DISH SERVINGS

1½ POUNDS SMALL RED POTATOES, EACH CUT INTO QUARTERS

1 JUMBO ONION (1 POUND), CUT INTO 8 WEDGES

6 TEASPOONS OLIVE OIL

¾ TEASPOON SALT

¼ TEASPOON COARSELY GROUND BLACK PEPPER

4 MEDIUM CHICKEN-BREAST HALVES, SKIN REMOVED

2 TABLESPOONS HONEY MUSTARD

1   Preheat oven to 450°F. In small roasting pan (13" by 9"), toss potatoes and onion with 4 teaspoons oil, salt, and pepper. Place pan on rack positioned in middle of oven and roast 25 minutes.

2   Meanwhile, place chicken-breast halves in second small roasting pan (13" by 9"); coat chicken with 1 teaspoon oil. In cup, mix remaining 1 teaspoon oil with honey mustard; set aside.

3   After potatoes and onions have baked 25 minutes, remove pan from oven and carefully turn pieces with metal spatula. Return to oven, placing pan on rack positioned in lower third of oven. Place chicken on rack positioned in upper third of oven.

4   After chicken has baked 10 minutes, brush with honey mustard mixture. Continue baking chicken, along with potatoes and onions, 12 to 15 minutes longer, until instant-read thermometer inserted horizontally into center of breast registers 165°F; potatoes and onions should be golden and tender. Serve hot.

380 **CALORIES** | **PER SERVING.** 31G PROTEIN | 44G CARBOHYDRATE | 10G TOTAL FAT (1G SATURATED) 5G FIBER | 66MG CHOLESTEROL | 630MG SODIUM 🌱

MAKE IT A MEAL: Serve with our Sesame Ginger Sprouts (65 calories; page 130) for a 445-calorie dinner, or with steamed haricot verts (40 calories), as shown in photo.

ROASTED LEMON CHICKEN

Lemons and herbs infuse this roasted chicken. Be sure to serve it with the flavorful pan juices.

ACTIVE TIME: 10 MINUTES · TOTAL TIME: 1 HOUR 10 MINUTES PLUS STANDING
MAKES: 4 MAIN-DISH SERVINGS

1   CHICKEN (3½ POUNDS)

3   LEMONS

2   TABLESPOONS CHOPPED FRESH CHIVES

1   TABLESPOON CHOPPED FRESH TARRAGON LEAVES

1   TABLESPOON OLIVE OIL OR BUTTER, SOFTENED

½   TEASPOON KOSHER SALT

¼   TEASPOON GROUND BLACK PEPPER

1   Preheat oven to 450°F. Remove bag with giblets and neck from chicken cavity; discard or reserve for another use. Place chicken, breast side up, on rack in small roasting pan (13" by 9").

2   From 1 lemon, grate 1 teaspoon peel. Place peel in small bowl; stir in chives, tarragon, and oil. With fingertips, gently separate skin from meat on chicken breast, then rub herb mixture on meat under skin. Cut all lemons into quarters. Place quarters from grated lemon inside chicken cavity; reserve remaining lemon quarters. Tie chicken legs together with string.

3   Sprinkle chicken with salt and pepper.

4   Roast chicken 30 minutes. Add reserved lemon quarters to pan, tossing with juices. Roast chicken 30 minutes longer, until instant-read thermometer inserted in thickest part of thigh registers 165°F.

5   When chicken is done, lift from roasting pan and tilt slightly to allow juices inside cavity to run into roasting pan.

6   Place chicken on platter. With slotted spoon, transfer roasted lemon quarters to platter with chicken. Let chicken stand 10 minutes to allow juices to set for easier carving. Skim and discard fat from pan juices. Serve chicken with roasted lemon wedges and pan juices.

360 CALORIES

PER SERVING. 37G PROTEIN | 6G CARBOHYDRATE | 22G TOTAL FAT (6G SATURATED) 3G FIBER | 146MG CHOLESTEROL | 350MG SODIUM

MAKE IT A MEAL: For a 505-calorie dinner, serve with our Vegetable-Herb Stuffing (90 calories; page 113) and Lemony Bean Duo (55 calories; page 126) on the side.

HOISIN-SESAME CHICKEN

These chicken thighs are brushed with hoisin sauce and sprinkled with sesame seeds before baking. A luscious hoisin and chili dipping sauce is served on the side.

ACTIVE TIME: 10 MINUTES · TOTAL TIME: 30 MINUTES
MAKES: 4 MAIN-DISH SERVINGS

8   SMALL BONE-IN CHICKEN THIGHS (2 POUNDS), SKIN AND FAT REMOVED (SEE TIP)

¼   CUP PLUS 2 TABLESPOONS HOISIN SAUCE

2   TABLESPOONS SESAME SEEDS

2   TABLESPOONS CHILI SAUCE

1½ TEASPOONS CHOPPED, PEELED FRESH GINGER

1½ TEASPOONS RICE VINEGAR

¼   TEASPOON CHINESE FIVE-SPICE POWDER

1   Preheat oven to 475°F.

2   Arrange chicken thighs in 15½" by 10½" jelly-roll pan. Into cup, pour ¼ cup hoisin sauce; use to brush both sides of thighs. Sprinkle with sesame seeds. Bake 20 to 25 minutes, until instant-read thermometer inserted into thickest part of thigh registers 165°F.

3   Meanwhile, prepare dipping sauce: In microwave-safe cup, combine chili sauce, ginger, vinegar, five-spice powder, and remaining 2 tablespoons hoisin sauce. Just before serving, heat mixture in microwave oven on High 45 seconds, stirring once. Serve chicken with dipping sauce.

TIP When removing the chicken skin, you'll get a good grip with less mess by holding the skin with a paper towel while peeling it away from the meat.

305 CALORIES

PER SERVING. 29G PROTEIN | 14G CARBOHYDRATE | 14G TOTAL FAT (4G SATURATED) 1G FIBER | 100MG CHOLESTEROL | 535MG SODIUM

MAKE IT A MEAL: For a casual 510-calorie summer dinner, serve the chicken atop 1 cup basmati rice (205 calories).

TURKEY BREAST WITH VEGETABLE GRAVY

We slimmed down this holiday centerpiece by serving a turkey breast without its skin, degreasing the drippings, and thickening the gravy with roasted vegetables—but your guests will never know it! Use the leftovers to make our yummy Turkey Leftovers Pie on page 61.

ACTIVE TIME: 40 MINUTES · TOTAL TIME: 2 HOURS 40 MINUTES PLUS STANDING
MAKES: 8 MAIN-DISH SERVINGS

1	BONE-IN TURKEY BREAST (6 POUNDS)	2	CARROTS, PEELED AND CUT INTO 3-INCH PIECES
½	TEASPOON SALT		
¼	TEASPOON GROUND BLACK PEPPER	3	GARLIC CLOVES, PEELED
2	MEDIUM ONIONS, EACH CUT INTO QUARTERS	½	TEASPOON DRIED THYME
		1	CAN (14½ OUNCES) CHICKEN BROTH
2	STALKS CELERY, CUT INTO 3-INCH PIECES	1	CUP WATER

1 Preheat oven to 350°F. Rinse turkey breast inside and out with cold running water and drain well. Pat dry with paper towels. Rub outside of turkey with salt and pepper.

2 Place turkey, skin side up, on rack in medium roasting pan (14" by 10").

3 Scatter onions, celery, carrots, garlic, and thyme around turkey in roasting pan. Cover turkey with loose tent of foil. Roast turkey 1 hour. Remove foil and roast 1 hour to 1 hour and 15 minutes longer, checking for doneness during last 30 minutes. Turkey breast is done when instant-read thermometer inserted in thickest part of breast (not touching bone) registers 165°F. Internal temperature of meat will rise to 170°F upon standing.

4 Transfer turkey to warm platter. Let stand 15 minutes for easier carving.

5 Meanwhile, prepare gravy: Remove rack from roasting pan. Pour vegetables and pan drippings into sieve set over 4-cup liquid measure or medium bowl; transfer solids to blender. Let juices stand until fat rises to top, about 1 minute. Skim and discard fat from drippings.

6 Add broth to hot roasting pan and heat to boiling, stirring until browned bits are loosened from bottom of pan. Pour broth mixture through sieve into pan juices in measuring cup.

7 In blender, puree reserved solids with pan juices and water until smooth. Pour puree into 2-quart saucepan; heat to boiling over high heat. Makes about 4 cups gravy.

8 To serve, remove skin from turkey. Serve sliced turkey with gravy.

285 CALORIES **PER SERVING TURKEY WITHOUT SKIN.** 63G PROTEIN | 0G CARBOHYDRATE 2G TOTAL FAT (1G SATURATED) | 0G FIBER | 174MG CHOLESTEROL | 255MG SODIUM

20 CALORIES **PER ½ CUP GRAVY.** 1G PROTEIN | 3G CARBOHYDRATE | 0G TOTAL FAT | 1G FIBER | 0MG CHOLESTEROL | 125MG SODIUM ♥

MAKE IT A MEAL: For a crowd-pleasing 465-calorie dinner, add Vegetable-Herb Stuffing (90 calories; page 113) and Honeyed Radishes and Turnips (80 calories; page 130).

MUSTARD-DILL SALMON WITH HERBED POTATOES

A light and creamy sauce adds piquant flavor to succulent salmon.

ACTIVE TIME: 20 MINUTES · **TOTAL TIME:** 30 MINUTES
MAKES: 4 MAIN-DISH SERVINGS

12 OUNCES SMALL RED POTATOES, CUT INTO 1-INCH CHUNKS

12 OUNCES SMALL WHITE POTATOES, CUT INTO 1-INCH CHUNKS

1½ TEASPOONS SALT

3 TABLESPOONS CHOPPED FRESH DILL

½ TEASPOON COARSELY GROUND BLACK PEPPER

4 PIECES SALMON FILLET (6 OUNCES EACH)

2 TABLESPOONS LIGHT MAYONNAISE

1 TABLESPOON WHITE WINE VINEGAR

2 TEASPOONS DIJON MUSTARD

¾ TEASPOON SUGAR

1 In a 3-quart saucepan, heat potatoes, 1 teaspoon salt, and enough *water* to cover to boiling over high heat. Reduce heat to low; cover and simmer until potatoes are fork-tender, about 15 minutes. Drain potatoes and toss with 1 tablespoon dill, ¼ teaspoon salt, and ¼ teaspoon pepper; keep potatoes warm.

2 Meanwhile, preheat boiler and place rack at closest position to heat source. Grease rack in broiling pan. Place salmon on rack; sprinkle with ⅛ teaspoon each salt and pepper. Broil until just opaque throughout, 8 to 10 minutes. (Instant-read thermometer inserted horizontally into salmon should register 145°F.)

3 While salmon is broiling, prepare sauce: In small bowl, mix mayonnaise, vinegar, mustard, sugar, remaining 2 tablespoons dill, and remaining ⅛ teaspoon each salt and pepper.

4 Serve salmon with sauce and potatoes.

335 CALORIES

PER SERVING. 37G PROTEIN | 31G CARBOHYDRATE | 7G TOTAL FAT (1G SATURATED)
2G FIBER | 86MG CHOLESTEROL | 655MG SODIUM

> **MAKE IT A MEAL:** After you make the mustard sauce, sauté snow peas in a nonstick skillet with 1 teaspoon vegetable oil for a healthy side dish (75 calories). Finish with our Raspberry Soufflé (75 calories; page 138) for a guest-worthy 485-calorie dinner.

COD WITH MUSHROOM RAGOUT

The rich earthiness of mushrooms meets mild cod to deliver an entrée that's low in calories.

ACTIVE TIME: 10 MINUTES · **TOTAL TIME:** 30 MINUTES

MAKES: 4 MAIN-DISH SERVINGS

1 LARGE SWEET POTATO, PEELED AND CUT INTO ½-INCH CHUNKS

2 TABLESPOONS EXTRA-VIRGIN OLIVE OIL

2 LARGE SHALLOTS, THINLY SLICED

½ TEASPOON SALT

½ TEASPOON GROUND BLACK PEPPER

2 PACKAGES (10 OUNCES EACH) SLICED MUSHROOMS

2 TABLESPOONS WATER

4 SKINLESS COD FILLETS (6 OUNCES EACH)

¼ CUP PACKED FRESH FLAT-LEAF PARSLEY LEAVES, FINELY CHOPPED

½ CUP DRY WHITE WINE

1   Preheat oven to 450°F.

2   On 18" by 12" jelly-roll pan, combine sweet potato, 1 tablespoon oil, half of shallots, and ⅛ teaspoon each salt and pepper. Arrange in single layer on one side of pan. Roast 15 minutes.

3   Meanwhile, in 12-inch skillet, heat remaining 1 tablespoon oil over medium-high. Add remaining shallot and cook 2 to 3 minutes or until tender and golden brown, stirring occasionally. Add mushrooms and water; cook 8 minutes or until liquid evaporates, stirring occasionally.

4   Arrange cod on other side of roasting pan. Sprinkle with ⅛ teaspoon each salt and pepper. Roast alongside potato 8 to 10 minutes or until fish is just opaque throughout. (Instant-read thermometer inserted horizontally into fish should register 145°F.)

5   Stir parsley, wine, and remaining ¼ teaspoon each salt and pepper into mushroom mixture. Cook 1 minute or until wine is reduced by half.

6   Divide potato and cod among serving plates. Spoon mushroom ragout over cod.

295 CALORIES

PER SERVING. 33G PROTEIN | 22G CARBOHYDRATE | 9G TOTAL FAT (1G SATURATED) 4G FIBER | 65MG CHOLESTEROL | 420MG SODIUM

MAKE IT A MEAL: Pair with our Creamed Spinach (180 calories; page 133) for a quick and easy 475-calorie dinner.

GLAZED MEAT LOAF

Adding ground turkey meat and oats to the traditional ground beef base makes this meat loaf lighter and healthier—but it's just as hearty and comforting as any old-fashioned recipe.

ACTIVE TIME: 35 MINUTES · TOTAL TIME: 1 HOUR 35 MINUTES
MAKES: 8 MAIN-DISH SERVINGS

1 CUP QUICK-COOKING OATS	¼ CUP PLUS 2 TABLESPOONS KETCHUP
½ CUP NONFAT MILK	1 POUND LEAN GROUND BEEF SIRLOIN (93%)
1 MEDIUM ONION, FINELY CHOPPED	
2 PINCHES SALT	1 POUND GROUND TURKEY BREAST
1 LARGE RED PEPPER, FINELY CHOPPED	3 MEDIUM CARROTS, GRATED
3 GARLIC CLOVES, CRUSHED WITH GARLIC PRESS	2 TABLESPOONS SPICY BROWN MUSTARD
2 TEASPOONS REDUCED-SODIUM SOY SAUCE	¼ TEASPOON GROUND BLACK PEPPER

1 Preheat oven to 400°F. Line jelly-roll pan with foil; lightly coat with nonstick cooking spray. In medium bowl, stir together oats and milk.

2 Coat bottom of 12-inch skillet with nonstick cooking spray; heat over medium. Add onion and pinch salt; cook 2 to 4 minutes or until onion softens, stirring occasionally. Add red pepper and garlic; cook 4 to 6 minutes or until pepper softens, stirring often. Transfer to medium bowl; refrigerate to cool.

3 Meanwhile, in small bowl, whisk together soy sauce and ¼ cup ketchup.

4 In large bowl, with hands, combine beef, turkey, carrots, oat mixture, cooled vegetable mixture, mustard, remaining 2 tablespoons ketchup, remaining pinch salt, and black pepper until mixed.

5 Form mixture into 8" by 4" loaf on prepared pan. Brush top and sides with soy ketchup. Bake 45 to 50 minutes, until instant-read thermometer inserted in center registers 165°F.

240 CALORIES **PER SERVING.** 25G PROTEIN | 17G CARBOHYDRATE | 8G TOTAL FAT (3G SATURATED) 3G FIBER | 65MG CHOLESTEROL | 360MG SODIUM ♥ 🍴

MAKE IT A MEAL: For a stick-to-your-ribs meat loaf dinner, serve with Mashed Potatoes with Browned Onions (175 calories; page 122) and steamed Brussels sprouts (30 calories). Total calories for the meal: just 455.

MEATBALLS IN SPICY TOMATO SAUCE

Dishes like meatballs and meat loaf are perfect vehicles for injecting whole-grain healthiness into your diet. Here, cracked wheat is added to the mix. The spicy tomato sauce is sprinkled with feta for Middle Eastern flair.

ACTIVE TIME: 35 MINUTES · TOTAL TIME: 55 MINUTES PLUS STANDING
MAKES: 6 MAIN-DISH SERVINGS

½ CUP COARSE CRACKED WHEAT	1 TABLESPOON OLIVE OIL
2¾ CUPS COLD WATER	2 LARGE GARLIC CLOVES, MINCED
1 ONION	¼ TEASPOON GROUND CINNAMON
1 POUND LEAN GROUND BEEF (90%), PREFERABLY SIRLOIN	⅛ TO ¼ TEASPOON CAYENNE (GROUND RED) PEPPER
¼ CUP LIGHTLY PACKED FRESH MINT LEAVES, CHOPPED, PLUS ¼ CUP, TORN	1 CAN (28 OUNCES) PLUM TOMATOES IN JUICE
1 LARGE EGG, LIGHTLY BEATEN	⅓ CUP GOLDEN RAISINS
1 TEASPOON GROUND CUMIN	3 TABLESPOONS CRUMBLED FETA CHEESE
1 TEASPOON SALT	
½ TEASPOON GROUND BLACK PEPPER	

1   Place cracked wheat in medium bowl; bring 2 cups water to a boil and pour over wheat. Cover bowl with plastic wrap and let stand 30 minutes. Pour into large sieve and drain.

2   Meanwhile, preheat oven to 400°F. Line 15½" by 10½" jelly-roll pan with foil and spray with nonstick cooking spray. On large holes of box grater, grate enough onion to make ¼ cup. Chop remaining onion and set aside.

3   In large bowl, combine cracked wheat, grated onion, beef, chopped mint, egg, ½ teaspoon cumin, ½ teaspoon salt, ¼ teaspoon black pepper, and ¼ cup cold water until well blended, but not overmixed.

4   Shape mixture by heaping tablespoonfuls into 24 meatballs. Place 1 inch apart on prepared pan. Bake until cooked through, about 20 minutes.

5   Meanwhile, in large heavy skillet over medium heat, heat oil until hot. Add reserved chopped onion and cook until tender and starting to brown, about 8 minutes, stirring often. Stir in garlic, cinnamon, cayenne, and remaining ½ teaspoon cumin, ½ teaspoon salt, and ¼ teaspoon black pepper; cook until fragrant, about 30 seconds. Add tomatoes with their juice, raisins, and remaining ½ cup water; bring to a boil over high heat, breaking up tomatoes with side of spoon. Reduce heat, cover, and simmer, stirring occasionally, until sauce thickens, about 20 minutes.

6 Add meatballs and simmer until meatballs are hot, about 5 minutes. Sprinkle with feta and torn mint leaves.

250 CALORIES **PER SERVING.** 20G PROTEIN | 24G CARBOHYDRATE | 8G TOTAL FAT (3G SATURATED) 4G FIBER | 80MG CHOLESTEROL | 776MG SODIUM

THE GROUND ROUNDUP

Supermarkets offer so many choices in ground meat and poultry. Here are flavor profiles and nutritional values to help you choose.

MEAT	FLAVOR PROFILE	APPROXIMATE NUTRITIONAL VALUES*	COOK-TO INTERNAL TEMPERATURE
Ground beef chuck, 80% lean	Juicy, rich, bold, robust, hearty	307 calories, 20g fat (8g saturated), 103mg cholesterol	160°F (medium doneness)
Ground lamb	Unique, full flavored, firm texture, aromatic	321 calories, 22g fat (9g saturated), 102mg cholesterol	160°F (medium doneness)
Ground pork	Delicate, mild, good alternative to beef and poultry	336 calories, 24g fat (9g saturated), 107mg cholesterol	160°F (medium doneness)
Ground chicken	Lean, light texture, tender, subtle flavor	172 calories, 11g fat (3g saturated), 65mg cholesterol	170°F (well-done)
Ground turkey	Moist, delicate flavor, denser than chicken	213 calories, 12g fat (3g saturated), 113mg cholesterol	170°F (well-done)

*Per 4-ounce cooked meat. Values vary among brands.

MAKE IT A MEAL: To up the fiber content even more, serve the meatballs and sauce over 1 cup whole-grain pasta (200 calories).

ROAST BEEF WITH HORSERADISH CREAM

A juicy seasoned sirloin tip roast is the centerpiece of this delicious meal. With a side of roasted potatoes, it's sure to become a family favorite. Serve it for dinner, or for a special occasion to feed a group.

ACTIVE TIME: 15 MINUTES · TOTAL TIME: 45 MINUTES
MAKES: 6 MAIN-DISH SERVINGS

---

4   GARLIC CLOVES

2   SPRIGS FRESH ROSEMARY

4   TEASPOONS OLIVE OIL

⅝   TEASPOON SALT

⅝   TEASPOON GROUND BLACK PEPPER

1½ POUNDS YUKON GOLD POTATOES, EACH CUT IN HALF (OR QUARTERS IF LARGE)

1   WHOLE (2- TO 2½-POUND) TRI-TIP (SIRLOIN TIP) ROAST, WELL TRIMMED

¼   CUP HEAVY CREAM

2   TABLESPOONS PREPARED HORSERADISH

½   TEASPOON DIJON MUSTARD

½   TEASPOON WHITE WINE VINEGAR

1 Preheat oven to 475°F. With side of chef's knife, gently smash 3 garlic cloves; discard peel. Into small bowl, crush remaining garlic clove with garlic press. Cut 1 rosemary sprig into 1-inch pieces; set aside. Remove leaves from other sprig; discard stem. Finely chop leaves and add to bowl with crushed garlic along with 1 teaspoon oil and ¼ teaspoon each salt and pepper; set aside.

2 In 18" by 12" jelly-roll pan, combine potatoes, remaining 3 teaspoons oil, smashed garlic cloves, snipped rosemary, and ¼ teaspoon each salt and pepper until well mixed. Spread in even layer, making space in center of pan for beef. Place beef in pan, fat side down; rub with reserved garlic-rosemary mixture.

3 Roast 20 minutes or until beef browns. Reset oven control to 350°F. Roast 8 to 10 minutes or until instant-read thermometer inserted into thickest part of beef registers 145°F; transfer to cutting board. Cover loosely; let stand 10 minutes. Transfer potatoes to platter.

4 Meanwhile, whisk cream, horseradish, mustard, vinegar, and remaining ⅛ teaspoon each salt and pepper until well blended. Slice meat thinly; serve with potatoes and horseradish cream.

360 PER SERVING. 32G PROTEIN | 16G CARBOHYDRATE | 19G TOTAL FAT (7G SATURATED)
CALORIES 2G FIBER | 84MG CHOLESTEROL | 335MG SODIUM

MAKE IT A MEAL: This roast with potatoes would pair beautifully with the slightly bitter flavor of broccoli rabe sautéed in 2 teaspoons extra-virgin olive oil (65 calories per serving) for a 425-calorie dinner.

SOY-HONEY PORK LOIN

Honey-soy glaze unites sweet potatoes and pork tenderloin for a very tasty low-calorie meal. For photo, see page 72.

ACTIVE TIME: 15 MINUTES · TOTAL TIME: 40 MINUTES PLUS MARINATING AND STANDING
MAKES: 4 MAIN-DISH SERVINGS

¼ CUP REDUCED-SODIUM SOY SAUCE

2 TABLESPOONS HOISIN SAUCE

2 TABLESPOONS HONEY

1 TABLESPOON RICE VINEGAR

1 TEASPOON GRATED, PEELED FRESH GINGER

2 GARLIC CLOVES, CRUSHED

1 WHOLE PORK TENDERLOIN (1¼ POUNDS)

1½ POUNDS SWEET POTATOES

1 TABLESPOON VEGETABLE OIL

¼ TEASPOON SALT

⅛ TEASPOON GROUND BLACK PEPPER

2 GREEN ONIONS, CUT INTO SLIVERS

1   Preheat oven to 475°F. In small bowl, whisk soy sauce, hoisin, honey, vinegar, ginger, and half of garlic. Pour into gallon-size zip-tight plastic bag. Add pork; seal bag and turn until pork is well coated. Set aside.

2   While pork marinates, peel sweet potatoes. Cut each into ½-inch-thick rounds. In large bowl, combine oil and remaining garlic. Add sweet potatoes, salt, and pepper. Toss until well coated.

3   Transfer pork from marinade to center of 18" by 12" jelly-roll pan, shaking any excess marinade off into bag. Tuck tapered ends under pork to ensure even cooking. Arrange sweet potato rounds in single layer on pan around pork. Roast 10 minutes.

4   Meanwhile, transfer marinade to 2-quart saucepan. Heat to boiling on medium-high. Boil 3 minutes or until syrupy. Transfer half of marinade to small serving bowl; set aside. Turn sweet potatoes and pork over. Brush remaining marinade on pork. Roast 10 to 15 minutes longer, until instant-read thermometer inserted into thickest part registers 145°F and sweet potatoes are browned. Cover pork loosely with foil and let stand 5 minutes.

5   Cut pork into ½-inch-thick slices. Transfer pork and sweet potatoes to large platter. Garnish with green onions and serve with reserved marinade.

345 CALORIES **PER SERVING.** 30G PROTEIN | 37G CARBOHYDRATE | 8G TOTAL FAT (2G SATURATED) 4G FIBER | 78MG CHOLESTEROL | 1,273MG SODIUM

MAKE IT A MEAL: Serve with Sesame Ginger Sprouts (65 calories; page 130) for a 410-calorie meal featuring Asian flavors.

MUSTARD-GLAZED FRESH HAM

The perfect centerpiece for a holiday buffet. Your guests may find it hard to believe that this luscious ham is less than 350 calories a serving, but it's true!

ACTIVE TIME: 20 MINUTES · TOTAL TIME: 4 HOURS 20 MINUTES PLUS STANDING
MAKES: 24 MAIN-COURSE SERVINGS

1	WHOLE (ABOUT 15 POUNDS) PORK LEG (BONE-IN FRESH HAM)	1	TEASPOON COARSELY GROUND BLACK PEPPER
½	CUP PACKED BROWN SUGAR	¼	TEASPOON GROUND CLOVES
1	TABLESPOON DRY MUSTARD	2½	CUPS APPLE CIDER
1	TABLESPOON KOSHER SALT		ROSEMARY SPRIGS FOR GARNISH

1 Preheat oven to 350°F. With knife, remove and discard skin from pork. Trim excess fat, leaving ¼-inch-thick layer of fat. Place pork on rack in large roasting pan (17" by 11½").

2 In small bowl, combine sugar, mustard, salt, pepper, and cloves. Rub mixture on top and sides of pork, pressing lightly so it adheres.

3 Roast pork 4 to 5 hours (16 to 20 minutes per pound), or until instant-read thermometer inserted in thickest part registers 160°F. (Meat near bone may still be slightly pink.) Temperature will rise to 165°F upon standing.

4 When roast is done, transfer to warm, large platter; let stand 20 minutes to set juices for easier carving.

5 Remove rack from roasting pan. Strain pan drippings into medium bowl. Let stand 1 minute, until fat separates. Skim and discard fat. Return pan drippings to hot roasting pan; add cider and heat to boiling over high heat, stirring until browned bits are loosened from bottom of pan. Boil about 7 minutes or until sauce thickens slightly. Strain sauce into gravy boat or serving bowl. Makes about 2¾ cups.

6 Thinly slice roast and serve with cider sauce. Garnish with rosemary.

340 CALORIES

PER SERVING WITH 1 TABLESPOON SAUCE. 30G PROTEIN | 7G CARBOHYDRATES 20G TOTAL FAT (7G SATURATED) | 0G FIBER | 107MG CHOLESTEROL | 300MG SODIUM

MAKE IT A MEAL: Sweet Potatoes with Marshmallow Meringue (100 calories; page 115) plus Apple Cider Greens (60 calories; page 128) makes for a festive 500-calorie dinner.

260
CALORIES

*Crustless Leek and
Gruyère Quiche
(page 100)*

BREAKFASTS & BRUNCHES

Our Steel-Cut Oatmeal plus three fruit and nut swirled variations are a wholesome and delicious jumpstart on busy mornings. But eggs are the ultimate A.M. comfort food, so we made sure to include lots of irresistible options. Our Crustless Leek and Gruyère Quiche is elegant brunch fare, while our Breakfast Tortilla Stack or Classic Cheese Omelet make an energizing start to any day. For a bistro-style meal, serve our Frisée Salad with a Poached Egg; it's tossed with a yummy bacon-shallot vinaigrette. Craving something sweet? Our Puffy Apple Pancake tastes like a decadent treat, but a serving costs you just 300 calories.

KEY TO ICONS

🕐 30 minutes or less ♥ Heart healthy 🌾 High fiber 🍱 Make ahead 🍲 Slow cooker

STEEL-CUT OATMEAL

If you haven't tried steel-cut oats, you're in for a deliciously chewy, full-flavored treat. We've included several tasty variations.

ACTIVE TIME: 5 MINUTES · TOTAL TIME: 30 MINUTES
MAKES: 4 MAIN-DISH SERVINGS

---

3 CUPS WATER

1 CUP STEEL-CUT OATS

PINCH SALT

In medium saucepan, combine water, oats, and salt. Bring to boiling over high heat. Reduce heat and cover. Simmer until water is absorbed and oats are tender but still chewy, 20 to 25 minutes, stirring occasionally.

75 CALORIES **PER SERVING.** 3G PROTEIN | 14G CARBOHYDRATE | 1G TOTAL FAT (0G SATURATED) 2G FIBER | 0MG CHOLESTEROL | 35MG SODIUM

BLUEBERRY-ALMOND OATMEAL

In small bowl, mix **1 cup fresh blueberries**, **¼ cup toasted and chopped almonds**, and **4 teaspoons honey**. Divide topping among servings of oatmeal.

95 CALORIES **PER SERVING.** 3G PROTEIN | 17G CARBOHYDRATE | 2G TOTAL FAT (0G SATURATED) 2G FIBER | 0MG CHOLESTEROL | 35MG SODIUM

CRANBERRY-WALNUT OATMEAL

In small bowl, mix **1 cup dried cranberries**, **1 cup chopped walnuts**, and **⅓ cup maple syrup**. Divide topping among servings of oatmeal.

165 CALORIES **PER SERVING.** 4G PROTEIN | 25G CARBOHYDRATE | 6G TOTAL FAT (1G SATURATED) 3G FIBER | 0MG CHOLESTEROL | 36MG SODIUM

APPLE-CINNAMON OATMEAL

Melt **1 tablespoon butter** in medium skillet over medium-high heat. Add **2 peeled, cored, and diced apples**. Reduce heat to medium; cook apples until tender, about 8 minutes, stirring a few times. Stir in ¼ **teaspoon ground cinnamon**. Divide apples among servings of oatmeal and sprinkle each bowl with **1 tablespoon brown sugar**.

190 CALORIES

PER SERVING. 3G PROTEIN | 37G CARBOHYDRATE | 4G TOTAL FAT (2G SATURATED) 3G FIBER | 8MG CHOLESTEROL | 59MG SODIUM

MAKE IT A MEAL: Serve the plain oatmeal or any of the variations with one hard-boiled egg (80 calories) and one-half red or pink grapefruit (50 calories) for a 205- to 320-calorie start to your day. Or enjoy a slice of our Banana Quick Bread (170 calories; page 121) with the plain oatmeal for 245 calories total.

CLASSIC CHEESE OMELET

Here's a classic omelet recipe to fill with your choice of shredded cheese. Because cooking time is so short, you'll need to have your eggs, seasonings, and fillings prepared and at your elbow so you can give individual attention to each omelet.

ACTIVE TIME: 5 MINUTES · TOTAL TIME: 20 MINUTES
MAKES: 4 MAIN-DISH SERVINGS

8 LARGE EGGS	4 OUNCES SHREDDED CHEDDAR, GRUYÈRE, OR FONTINA CHEESE (1 CUP)
½ CUP WATER	
½ TEASPOON SALT	CHOPPED GREEN ONIONS
½ TEASPOON GROUND BLACK PEPPER	TOASTED COUNTRY-STYLE BREAD (OPTIONAL)
2 TABLESPOONS BUTTER OR MARGARINE	

1   Preheat oven to 200°F.

2   Place dinner plates in oven to warm. In medium bowl, place eggs, water, salt, and pepper. With fork, beat 25 to 30 quick strokes to blend mixture without making it fluffy. (Overbeating eggs toughens proteins in whites.)

3   In nonstick 8-inch skillet, melt ½ tablespoon butter over medium heat. When butter stops sizzling, pour or ladle ½ cup egg mixture into skillet.

4   After egg mixture begins to set around edges, about 25 to 30 seconds, with heat-safe spatula, carefully push cooked egg from side of skillet toward center, so uncooked egg can reach bottom of hot skillet. Repeat 8 to 10 times around skillet, tilting as necessary, 1 to 1½ minutes.

5   Cook until omelet is almost set but still creamy and moist on top. Place skillet handle facing you, and sprinkle ¼ cup cheese on half of omelet.

6   With spatula, fold omelet in half, covering cheese.

7   Shake pan gently to loosen any egg or cheese from edge, then slide omelet to edge of skillet.

8   Holding skillet above warm plate, tip skillet so omelet slides onto plate. Put plate in oven to keep omelet warm. Repeat with remaining butter, egg mixture, and cheese to make 4 omelets in all. Sprinkle with green onions. Serve with toast, if desired.

315
CALORIES

PER OMELET. 20G PROTEIN | 2G CARBOHYDRATE | 25G TOTAL FAT (10G SATURATED)
0G FIBER | 455MG CHOLESTEROL | 670MG SODIUM

MAKE IT A MEAL: A Dill-Pepper Buttermilk Biscuit (60 calories; page 112) or one-half small apple plus two teaspoons peanut butter (100 calories) makes for a power breakfast (375 or 415 calories respectively).

BREAKFAST TORTILLA STACK

Need a breakfast that will keep you full all morning long? Top a whole-wheat tortilla with fluffy eggs, fat-free refried beans, and flavorful salsa.

ACTIVE TIME: 25 MINUTES · TOTAL TIME: 30 MINUTES
MAKES: 4 MAIN-DISH SERVINGS

¼ CUP CHOPPED RED ONION	⅛ TEASPOON SALT
2 RIPE MEDIUM TOMATOES (6 TO 8 OUNCES EACH), CHOPPED	⅛ TEASPOON GROUND BLACK PEPPER
	1 CUP FAT-FREE REFRIED BEANS
¼ CUP LOOSELY PACKED FRESH CILANTRO LEAVES, CHOPPED	¼ TEASPOON GROUND CHIPOTLE CHILE
4 LARGE EGGS	4 (7-INCH) WHOLE-WHEAT TORTILLAS
4 LARGE EGG WHITES	

1 In 1 *cup ice water,* soak chopped onion 10 minutes; drain well. In small bowl, combine onion, tomatoes, and cilantro; set aside.

2 In medium bowl, with wire whisk or fork, beat whole eggs, egg whites, salt, and pepper until blended.

3 Spray nonstick 10-inch skillet with cooking spray; heat on medium 1 minute. Pour egg mixture into skillet; cook about 5 minutes or until egg mixture is set but still moist, stirring occasionally.

4 Meanwhile, in microwave-safe small bowl, mix beans and chipotle chile. Cover with vented plastic wrap; heat in microwave on High 1 minute or until hot.

5 Place stack of tortillas between damp paper towels on microwave-safe plate; heat in microwave on High 10 to 15 seconds to warm. To serve, layer each tortilla with eggs, beans, and salsa.

200 CALORIES

PER SERVING. 13G PROTEIN | 29G CARBOHYDRATE | 4G TOTAL FAT (1G SATURATED) 13G FIBER | 160MG CHOLESTEROL | 635MG SODIUM

MAKE IT A MEAL: Want to serve this for brunch? Add a side of Ginger-Jalapeño Slaw (65 calories; page 129) and half a pink grapefruit (50 calories) for a 315-calorie meal.

HUEVOS RANCHEROS

Fast and flavorful, these Mexican-inspired baked eggs are ideal for brunch. Baking rather than frying the tortilla cups keeps the calories and fat in check.

ACTIVE TIME: 15 MINUTES · TOTAL TIME: 40 MINUTES
MAKES: 4 MAIN-DISH SERVINGS

4   (6-INCH) CORN TORTILLAS

NONSTICK COOKING SPRAY

1   JAR (16 OUNCES) MILD LOW-SODIUM SALSA

1   CUP CANNED BLACK BEANS, RINSED AND DRAINED

1   CUP FROZEN CORN KERNELS

3   GREEN ONIONS, SLICED

1   TEASPOON GROUND CUMIN

4   LARGE EGGS

½   CUP LOOSELY PACKED FRESH CILANTRO LEAVES, THINLY SLICED

½   AVOCADO, SLICED INTO THIN WEDGES

1   Preheat oven to 350°F. On 15½" by 10½" jelly-roll pan, invert four 6-ounce custard cups. With kitchen shears, make four evenly spaced 1-inch cuts, from edge toward center, around each tortilla. Lightly spray both sides of tortillas with cooking spray and drape each over a custard cup. Bake tortilla cups 8 minutes or until golden and crisp.

2   Meanwhile, in nonstick 12-inch skillet, combine salsa, beans, corn, green onions, and cumin; heat to boiling over medium heat. Cover and cook 3 minutes to blend flavors.

3   With large spoon, make four indentations in salsa mixture, spaced evenly around skillet. One at a time, break eggs into cup and gently pour into indentations. Cover and simmer 8 to 10 minutes or until eggs are set or cooked to desired doneness.

4   To serve, set each tortilla cup on plate. Spoon egg with some salsa mixture into each tortilla cup. Spoon any remaining salsa mixture around and on eggs in cups. Sprinkle with cilantro; serve with avocado wedges.

290 CALORIES | **PER SERVING.** 12G PROTEIN | 40G CARBOHYDRATE | 10G TOTAL FAT (2G SATURATED) 11G FIBER | 213MG CHOLESTEROL | 630MG SODIUM

MAKE IT A MEAL: Finish this Mexican-style brunch favorite with our zesty Lime Triangles (95 calories each; page 140) for a 385-calorie meal.

BACON AND EGGS OVER ASPARAGUS

Here's a bistro-style take on classic bacon and eggs served over roasted thyme-scented asparagus.

ACTIVE TIME: 8 MINUTES · TOTAL TIME: 30 MINUTES

MAKES: 4 MAIN-DISH SERVINGS

8	SLICES BACON	8	LARGE EGGS
1	POUND ASPARAGUS SPEARS, TRIMMED	⅛	TEASPOON SALT
½	TEASPOON FRESH THYME LEAVES, CHOPPED	3	TABLESPOONS PACKED FRESH FLAT-LEAF PARSLEY LEAVES, CHOPPED
⅜	TEASPOON GROUND BLACK PEPPER	1	TABLESPOON FRESH DILL, CHOPPED

1   Preheat oven to 475°F. In 18" by 12" jelly-roll pan, arrange bacon slices in single layer, spacing ¼ inch apart. Roast 8 to 9 minutes or until browned and crisp. Transfer to paper-towel-lined plate; set aside. Drain and discard excess bacon fat in pan, leaving thin film of fat.

2   Add asparagus to pan in single layer. Roll in fat until evenly coated. Arrange so that bottoms of spears touch one long side of pan. Sprinkle thyme and ¼ teaspoon pepper on asparagus. Roast 8 to 10 minutes or until asparagus spears are tender and browned.

3   Carefully crack eggs, without breaking yolks (see Tip), directly onto asparagus spears, staggering if necessary and spacing ¼ inch apart. Carefully return pan to oven. Roast 5 to 6 minutes or until whites are just set and yolks are still runny. Sprinkle salt and remaining ⅛ teaspoon pepper on eggs. Return bacon to pan; sprinkle eggs and asparagus with parsley and dill. To serve, use wide spatula to transfer to individual serving plates.

TIP If you're worried about breaking the egg yolks, crack each egg, one at a time, into a small cup or bowl before pouring it onto the asparagus.

235 CALORIES

PER SERVING. 18G PROTEIN | 4G CARBOHYDRATE | 16G TOTAL FAT (5G SATURATED) 1G FIBER | 435MG CHOLESTEROL | 405MG SODIUM ♥

MAKE IT A MEAL: For a 345-calorie breakfast or brunch, add on a slice of whole-wheat toast with 1 teaspoon trans-fat-free margarine (110 calories).

THE NUTRITIONAL BENEFITS OF EGGS

Eggs got a bum rap for years. Yes, the yolk of an egg does contain cholesterol, but as hundreds of studies can attest, if eaten in moderation, eggs won't raise a person's overall cholesterol level. And eggs have so much to offer nutritionally. A single egg is a good source of selenium, which provides antioxidant protection; iodine, vital to thyroid function; energy-producing vitamin B_2; and protein.

CRUSTLESS LEEK AND GRUYÈRE QUICHE

This delicate custard is so smooth and tasty, you'll never miss the pastry. And did we mention that by losing it, we've saved you 200 calories and 13 grams of fat per serving? For photo, see page 90.

ACTIVE TIME: 20 MINUTES · TOTAL TIME: 50 MINUTES
MAKES: 6 MAIN-DISH SERVINGS

1 POUND LEEKS	1 TABLESPOON CORNSTARCH
1 TABLESPOON OLIVE OIL	¼ TEASPOON COARSELY GROUND BLACK PEPPER
½ TEASPOON SALT	
6 LARGE EGGS	4 OUNCES GRUYÈRE CHEESE, SHREDDED (1 CUP)
2½ CUPS WHOLE MILK	

1 Preheat oven to 350°F. Grease 10-inch quiche dish or 9½-inch deep-dish pie plate. Cut off roots and dark green tops from leeks; discard any tough outer leaves. Cut each leek lengthwise in half, then crosswise into ¼-inch-wide slices. Rinse leeks in large bowl of cold water, swishing to remove sand. With hands, transfer leeks to colander to drain, leaving sand in bottom of bowl. Repeat process, changing water several times, until all sand is removed. Shake colander to remove excess water from leeks.

2 In nonstick 12-inch skillet, heat oil on medium. Add leeks and ¼ teaspoon salt and cook 12 to 14 minutes or until leeks are tender and browned, stirring often. Transfer leeks to quiche dish; spread evenly.

3 Meanwhile, in bowl, with wire whisk, beat eggs, milk, cornstarch, pepper, and remaining ¼ teaspoon salt until well blended.

4 Pour egg mixture over leeks in dish. Sprinkle with Gruyère. Bake 30 to 35 minutes or until knife inserted in center comes out clean. Cool on wire rack for 5 minutes.

260 CALORIES

PER SERVING. 16G PROTEIN | 11G CARBOHYDRATE | 17G TOTAL FAT (8G SATURATED) 1G FIBER | 247MG CHOLESTEROL | 375MG SODIUM

MAKE IT A MEAL: Add on Oven Fries (130 calories; page 118) for a thoroughly satisfying brunch that's a surprising 390 calories total.

OVERNIGHT SAVORY FRENCH TOAST

This savory take on French toast feeds eight people—and the cheese-crusted combo of bread, eggs, and Gruyère rests in the refrigerator overnight so you can sleep in.

ACTIVE TIME: 15 MINUTES · TOTAL TIME: 1 HOUR 5 MINUTES PLUS CHILLING AND STANDING

MAKES: 8 MAIN-DISH SERVINGS

6   LARGE EGGS

2   CUPS MILK

1   TABLESPOON DIJON MUSTARD

¼   TEASPOON SALT

¼   TEASPOON GROUND BLACK PEPPER

¼   CUP SNIPPED FRESH CHIVES PLUS ADDITIONAL FOR GARNISH

1   LOAF (9 OUNCES) FRENCH BREAD (PREFERABLY DAY-OLD)

6   OUNCES GRUYÈRE CHEESE, SHREDDED (1½ CUPS)

1   Grease shallow 1½-quart ceramic baking dish. In medium bowl, whisk eggs, milk, mustard, salt, and pepper until well blended. Stir in chives.

2   Cut bread into ¼-inch-thick slices. Arrange half of slices in bottom of prepared baking dish, overlapping to fit. Pour half of egg mixture over bread and sprinkle with two-thirds of Gruyère. Cover with remaining bread, over-lapping slices. Pour remaining egg mixture over bread; gently press down to help bread absorb egg mixture. Sprinkle with remaining one-third of Gruyère. Cover and refrigerate overnight.

3   Preheat oven to 350°F. Bake 50 to 60 minutes or until puffed and golden and tip of knife inserted in center comes out clean, covering top during last 15 minutes if browning too quickly. Let stand 10 minutes to set custard before serving. Sprinkle with snipped chives.

355 CALORIES

PER SERVING. 22G PROTEIN | 20G CARBOHYDRATE | 20G TOTAL FAT (11G SATURATED) 1G FIBER | 214MG CHOLESTEROL | 495MG SODIUM

MAKE IT A MEAL: For added protein, serve with a Jimmy Dean turkey sausage link (55 calories) for a 410-calorie meal.

HAM AND CHEESE SOUFFLÉ

Ham and pepper Jack cheese partner up in this light and fluffy soufflé that can be served for brunch or dinner with a simple green salad.

ACTIVE TIME: 20 MINUTES · TOTAL TIME: 1 HOUR 10 MINUTES
MAKES: 6 MAIN-DISH SERVINGS

4   TABLESPOONS BUTTER OR MARGARINE

¼   CUP ALL-PURPOSE FLOUR

1½ CUPS REDUCED-FAT MILK (2%), WARMED

6   OUNCES PEPPER JACK CHEESE, SHREDDED (1½ CUPS)

4   LARGE EGGS, SEPARATED

3   OUNCES SMOKED HAM, CHOPPED (½ CUP)

1   CAN (4½ OUNCES) CHOPPED MILD GREEN CHILES, DRAINED

1   LARGE EGG WHITE

1   Preheat oven to 325°F. Grease 2-quart soufflé dish.

2   In heavy 2-quart saucepan, melt butter over low heat. Add flour and cook 1 minute, stirring. With wire whisk, gradually mix in milk. Cook over medium heat, stirring constantly, until sauce thickens and boils.

3   Reduce heat to low and simmer 3 minutes, stirring frequently. Stir in Pepper Jack and cook, stirring constantly, just until sauce is smooth. Remove saucepan from heat.

4   In medium bowl, with whisk, lightly beat egg yolks; gradually whisk in hot cheese sauce. Stir in ham and chiles.

5   In large bowl, with mixer on high speed, beat all egg whites until stiff peaks form when beaters are lifted. With rubber spatula, gently fold one-third of beaten egg whites into cheese mixture. Fold in remaining whites just until blended.

6   Pour mixture into prepared soufflé dish. Bake about 50 minutes or until soufflé is puffed and golden brown and knife inserted 1 inch from edge comes out clean. Serve immediately.

295 CALORIES

PER SERVING. 17G PROTEIN | 9G CARBOHYDRATE | 22G TOTAL FAT (9G SATURATED)
1G FIBER | 183MG CHOLESTEROL | 595MG SODIUM

MAKE IT A MEAL: Add a simple green salad with 2 tablespoons reduced-fat dressing (75 calories) and one of our Corn Muffins (145 calories; page 119) for a 515-calorie country-style meal.

POTATO PANCAKES WITH CARROT SALAD

To add a little color to these pancakes, substitute 1 cup shredded raw zucchini for an equal amount of hash brown potatoes. Scrub the zucchini first and pat it dry—but don't peel off the pretty green skin.

TOTAL TIME: 25 MINUTES

MAKES: 4 MAIN-DISH SERVINGS

CARROT SALAD

1   PACKAGE (10 OUNCES) SHREDDED CARROTS

1   CUP PACKED FRESH PARSLEY LEAVES

1   TABLESPOON FRESH LEMON JUICE

1   TABLESPOON EXTRA-VIRGIN OLIVE OIL

¼   TEASPOON SALT

POTATO PANCAKES

½   CUP VEGETABLE OIL

1   TEASPOON SALT

⅛   TEASPOON GROUND BLACK PEPPER

2   LARGE EGGS

1   BAG (20 OUNCES) REFRIGERATED SHREDDED HASH BROWN POTATOES (4 CUPS)

2   GREEN ONIONS, THINLY SLICED

1   Preheat oven to 200°F. Line cookie sheet with paper towels.

2   Meanwhile, prepare salad: In bowl, toss carrots, parsley, lemon juice, oil, and salt.

3   Prepare potato pancakes: In 12-inch skillet, heat oil over medium-high heat until very hot. In bowl, mix salt, pepper, and eggs. Add potatoes and green onions and stir until well mixed.

4   Drop mixture by scant ½ cups into hot oil to make 4 pancakes; flatten each into 4-inch oval. Cook until golden on both sides, 5 to 7 minutes. With slotted spatula, transfer pancakes to cookie sheet; keep warm in oven. Repeat with remaining mixture to make 8 pancakes.

5   Serve each pancake with carrot salad on the side.

315 CALORIES

PER SERVING. 8G PROTEIN | 38G CARBOHYDRATE | 15G TOTAL FAT (2G SATURATED) 5G FIBER | 93MG CHOLESTEROL | 912MG SODIUM

MAKE IT A MEAL: If you like, top the pancakes with ¼ cup unsweetened applesauce (25 calories) or 2 tablespoons reduced-fat sour cream (40 calories).

PUFFY APPLE PANCAKE

When you want pancakes, these skillet-browned apples topped with a light batter and baked are a great low-calorie option.

COOK TIME: 45 MINUTES · TOTAL TIME: 45 MINUTES
MAKES: 6 MAIN-DISH SERVINGS

2 TABLESPOONS BUTTER OR MARGARINE	3 LARGE EGGS
½ CUP PLUS 2 TABLESPOONS SUGAR	¾ CUP MILK
¼ CUP WATER	¾ CUP ALL-PURPOSE FLOUR
6 MEDIUM GRANNY SMITH OR NEWTOWN PIPPIN APPLES (ABOUT 2 POUNDS), PEELED, CORED, AND EACH CUT INTO 8 WEDGES	¼ TEASPOON SALT

1 Preheat oven to 425°F. In 12-inch skillet with oven-safe handle, heat butter, ½ cup sugar, and water to boiling over medium-high heat. Add apple wedges; cook about 15 minutes, stirring occasionally, until apples are golden and sugar mixture begins to caramelize.

2 Meanwhile, in blender on medium speed or in food processor with knife blade attached, blend eggs, milk, flour, salt, and remaining 2 tablespoons sugar until batter is smooth.

3 When apple mixture in skillet is golden and lightly caramelized, pour batter over apples. Place skillet in oven; bake pancake 15 minutes or until puffed and golden. Serve immediately.

300 CALORIES **PER SERVING.** 6G PROTEIN | 54G CARBOHYDRATE | 8G TOTAL FAT (1G SATURATED) 3G FIBER | 121 MG CHOLESTEROL | 181MG SODIUM ♥

MAKE IT A MEAL: Top each serving with ½ cup mixed berries plus 1 tablespoon maple syrup (85 calories) for a 385-calorie meal.

FRISÉE SALAD WITH A POACHED EGG

This delicious bistro-style dish tops a bacon and shallot vinaigrette tossed salad with a poached egg. For the salad, use frisée, a member of the chicory family with feathery leaves and a mildly bitter flavor, or mixed baby greens.

ACTIVE TIME: 10 MINUTES · **TOTAL TIME:** 20 MINUTES
MAKES: 6 MAIN-DISH SERVINGS

3   SLICES BACON, CUT INTO ½-INCH PIECES

12 OUNCES FRISÉE OR 2 BAGS (5 TO 6 OUNCES EACH) MIXED BABY SALAD GREENS

1   MEDIUM SHALLOT, MINCED

2   TABLESPOONS WHITE WINE VINEGAR

1   TEASPOON DIJON MUSTARD

¼   TEASPOON SALT

¼   TEASPOON COARSELY GROUND BLACK PEPPER PLUS MORE FOR SERVING

2   TABLESPOONS OLIVE OIL

6   LARGE EGGS

1   In 2-quart saucepan, cook bacon on medium 5 minutes or until browned, stirring occasionally.

2   Meanwhile, in 12-inch skillet, heat 1 *inch water* to boiling on high to poach eggs in later. Trim and discard stem ends from frisée; cut leaves into bite-size pieces. Place greens in large bowl.

3   Remove saucepan from heat. With slotted spoon, transfer bacon to paper towels to drain; discard all but 1 tablespoon bacon fat.

4   Into bacon fat remaining in skillet, whisk shallot, vinegar, mustard, salt, and ¼ teaspoon pepper. In slow, steady stream, whisk in oil until combined. Add warm vinaigrette to bowl with frisée and toss until evenly coated.

5   Reduce skillet heat to medium to maintain water at gentle simmer. Break eggs, one at a time, into cup. Holding cup close to surface of water, slip in each egg. Cook eggs 3 to 5 minutes or until whites are set and yolks begin to thicken. With slotted spoon, lift out each egg and quickly drain, still in spoon, on paper towels.

6   To serve, divide frisée among salad plates; top with bacon and egg. Sprinkle egg with black pepper.

170 CALORIES **PER SERVING.** 8G PROTEIN | 4G CARBOHYDRATE | 13G TOTAL FAT (4G SATURATED) 2G FIBER | 216MG CHOLESTEROL | 315MG SODIUM ⌄

MAKE IT A MEAL: Serve one of our Oatmeal Sconuts (235 calories; page 123) on the side for a 405-calorie brunch or lunch.

IRRESISTIBLE ADD-ONS

To make your meal planning a breeze, we've organized the add-on recipes in the following chapters by calorie count—from lowest to highest. Choose your main dish from the preceding chapters, then select one or more of these tempting add-ons. So, if you're preparing our Mustard-Glazed Fresh Ham (340 calories), you could add on our Light Potato Salad (160 calories) to create a 500-calorie dinner. Or you could enjoy two lower-calorie add-ons instead: Sweet Potatoes with Marshmallow Meringue (100 calories) plus Apple Cider Greens (60 calories)—and your meal will still add up to 500 calories total. It's that easy!

90
CALORIES
Vegetable-Herb Stuffing
(page 113)

POTATOES, BREADS & STUFFINGS

Mashed potatoes, corn bread, stuffing—sometimes the main dish is just an excuse to dig into comforting sides like these. We offer skinny takes on all of the above, plus lighter versions of potato skins, featuring reduced-fat sour cream and Pecorino; potato salad, utilizing low-fat buttermilk and light mayonnaise; and baked rather than fried French fries. Enjoy our dill buttermilk biscuits with a bowl of soup or, for breakfast, try our whole-wheat banana bread or oatmeal sconuts, a tantalizing cross between scones and doughnuts.

KEY TO ICONS

🕐 30 minutes or less   ♥ Heart healthy   ❂ High fiber   ▦ Make ahead   ⛁ Slow cooker

DILL-PEPPER BUTTERMILK BISCUITS

These easy, savory biscuits go well with salads, soups, and stews. Pop leftovers into a zip-seal bag and freeze up to one month; reheat in the toaster oven.

ACTIVE TIME: 15 MINUTES · **TOTAL TIME:** 30 MINUTES
MAKES: 24 BISCUITS

2 CUPS ALL-PURPOSE FLOUR

2½ TEASPOONS BAKING POWDER

½ TEASPOON BAKING SODA

½ TEASPOON GROUND BLACK PEPPER

¼ TEASPOON SALT

¼ CUP VEGETABLE SHORTENING

¾ CUP BUTTERMILK

3 TABLESPOONS CHOPPED FRESH DILL

1 Preheat oven to 450°F. In large bowl, combine flour, baking powder, baking soda, pepper, and salt. With pastry blender or two knives used scissors-fashion, cut in shortening until mixture resembles coarse crumbs. In cup, combine buttermilk and dill; stir into flour mixture just until mixture forms soft dough that leaves side of bowl.

2 Turn dough onto lightly floured surface; knead 6 to 8 times or just until smooth. With floured rolling pin, roll dough ¼ inch thick.

3 With floured 2-inch biscuit cutter, cut out rounds without twisting cutter. Arrange biscuits on ungreased cookie sheet, 1 inch apart.

4 Press trimmings together; reroll and cut out additional biscuits. Bake 12 to 14 minutes or until golden. Serve warm.

60 CALORIES

PER BISCUIT. 1G PROTEIN | 9G CARBOHYDRATE | 2G TOTAL FAT (1G SATURATED) 0G FIBER | 0MG CHOLESTEROL | 100MG SODIUM ♥ ♥

VEGETABLE-HERB STUFFING

Here's a classic stuffing to enjoy on holidays or whenever you have the craving. For photo, see page 110.

ACTIVE TIME: 20 MINUTES · **TOTAL TIME:** 1 HOUR 20 MINUTES
MAKES: 24 SIDE-DISH SERVINGS

- 12 OUNCES SLICED FIRM WHITE BREAD
- 1 TABLESPOON OLIVE OIL
- 1 CARROT, FINELY CHOPPED
- 1 STALK CELERY, FINELY CHOPPED
- 1 SMALL ONION, FINELY CHOPPED
- ¼ CUP LOOSELY PACKED FRESH PARSLEY LEAVES, COARSELY CHOPPED
- ½ TEASPOON POULTRY SEASONING
- ¼ TEASPOON SALT
- ⅛ TEASPOON GROUND BLACK PEPPER
- 1¼ CUPS CANNED CHICKEN BROTH

1 Preheat oven to 400°F. Grease shallow 1½- to 2-quart baking dish and set aside.

2 Arrange bread slices on a large cookie sheet and toast in oven 16 to 17 minutes or until golden and dry, turning over halfway through toasting.

3 Meanwhile, in nonstick 10-inch skillet, heat oil over medium heat until hot. Add carrot, celery, and onion and cook, stirring occasionally, until vegetables are tender and lightly browned, about 12 minutes.

4 Remove skillet from heat, then stir in parsley, poultry seasoning, salt, and pepper.

5 With serrated knife, cut toasted bread into ½-inch cubes, then place in very large bowl. Reset oven control to 325°F.

6 Add broth and vegetable mixture to bread in bowl and toss until bread is evenly moistened.

7 Spoon stuffing into prepared baking dish. Cover with foil and bake 30 minutes. Remove foil and bake 15 to 20 minutes longer or until heated through and lightly browned on top.

90 CALORIES **PER ½-CUP SERVING.** 3G PROTEIN | 16G CARBOHYDRATE | 2G TOTAL FAT (0G SATURATED) | 1G FIBER | 0MG CHOLESTEROL | 270MG SODIUM ♥

SWEET POTATOES WITH MARSHMALLOW MERINGUE

To modernize this crowd-pleaser, we microwaved the potatoes before mashing and topped them with meringue mounds—a less-sugary substitute for the mini marshmallows made popular in the 1950s.

ACTIVE TIME: 30 MINUTES · **TOTAL TIME:** 50 MINUTES
MAKES: 12 SIDE-DISH SERVINGS

3 POUNDS SWEET POTATOES	¼ TEASPOON SALT
2 TABLESPOONS PURE MAPLE SYRUP	3 LARGE EGG WHITES
1 TABLESPOON PACKED DARK BROWN SUGAR	¼ TEASPOON CREAM OF TARTAR
1 TABLESPOON FRESH LEMON JUICE	⅓ CUP GRANULATED SUGAR
⅛ TEASPOON GROUND ALLSPICE	

1   Preheat oven to 400°F. Pierce sweet potatoes all over with tip of knife; place in large microwave-safe bowl. Cover with vented plastic wrap and microwave on High 15 to 17 minutes or until very tender when pierced with fork; drain. When cool enough to handle, peel potatoes and return to bowl.

2   To bowl with sweet potatoes, add maple syrup, brown sugar, lemon juice, allspice, and salt. Mash potatoes with potato masher until smooth. Transfer to 2-quart casserole dish. (If making ahead, cover and refrigerate up to overnight, then bake in 400°F oven for 15 minutes or until heated through.)

3   Prepare meringue: In large bowl, with mixer on high speed, beat egg whites and cream of tartar until soft peaks form. Sprinkle in granulated sugar, 2 tablespoons at a time, beating until sugar dissolves and meringue stands in stiff, glossy peaks when beaters are lifted.

4   Transfer meringue to large piping bag fitted with ½-inch plain tip or to heavy-duty gallon-size zip-tight plastic bag with one corner cut to form ½-inch hole. Starting at one side of casserole dish, pipe meringue in small mounds onto surface of sweet potatoes, covering entire surface. Bake 6 to 8 minutes or until meringue is golden.

100 CALORIES — **PER SERVING.** 2G PROTEIN | 23G CARBOHYDRATE | 0G TOTAL FAT | 2G FIBER
0MG CHOLESTEROL | 90MG SODIUM

SLIMMED-DOWN POTATO SKINS

Our version of these tasty apps weighs in at just 120 calories per serving—versus the classic's 350—and has one-fifth the saturated fat. Our secret? Lighter ingredients (reduced-fat sour cream, Pecorino cheese) that pack a lot of flavor.

ACTIVE TIME: 35 MINUTES · **TOTAL TIME:** 1 HOUR 10 MINUTES
MAKES: 8 APPETIZER SERVINGS

4   LARGE BAKING POTATOES (12 OUNCES EACH), WELL SCRUBBED

4   SLICES CENTER-CUT BACON

1   TABLESPOON EXTRA-VIRGIN OLIVE OIL

⅛   TEASPOON SALT

⅛   TEASPOON GROUND BLACK PEPPER

⅓   CUP REDUCED-FAT SOUR CREAM

1   OUNCE PECORINO ROMANO CHEESE, FINELY GRATED

1   LARGE RIPE TOMATO (10 TO 12 OUNCES), FINELY CHOPPED

2   TABLESPOONS SNIPPED FRESH CHIVES

1   Preheat oven to 400°F.

2   With fork, pierce each potato three times. Place potatoes on parchment paper. Microwave on High 8 minutes. Turn over; microwave on High 10 minutes longer or until tender. Cover with kitchen towel; let cool.

3   Meanwhile, in 18" by 12" jelly-roll pan, arrange bacon in single layer. Roast 10 to 12 minutes or until browned and crisp. Drain on paper towels. When cool, crumble. Discard fat from pan but do not wipe clean; set pan aside. Reset oven control to 475°F.

4   Cut each potato in quarters lengthwise. With spoon, scoop potato from skins, leaving about ¼ inch of potato with skin and being careful not to break through skin. Reserve cooked potato flesh for another use.

5   Arrange skins, skin side up, in single layer on reserved pan. Brush with oil; sprinkle with salt and pepper.

6   Roast 13 to 15 minutes or until browned and crisp. Transfer, skin sides down, to serving plate.

7   To assemble, spread 1 teaspoon sour cream on each skin. Top with Pecorino, tomato, bacon, and chives.

120 CALORIES **PER SERVING.** 4G PROTEIN | 16G CARBOHYDRATE | 5G TOTAL FAT (2G SATURATED) 3G FIBER | 13MG CHOLESTEROL | 160MG SODIUM ♥

OVEN FRIES

You won't miss the fat in these hand-cut "fries." They bake beautifully with a spritz of nonstick cooking spray and a sprinkle of salt and pepper.

ACTIVE TIME: 10 MINUTES · **TOTAL TIME:** 30 MINUTES
MAKES: 4 SIDE-DISH SERVINGS

NONSTICK COOKING SPRAY

3   MEDIUM BAKING POTATOES
(8 OUNCES EACH)

½   TEASPOON SALT

¼   TEASPOON COARSELY
GROUND BLACK PEPPER

1   Preheat oven to 500°F. Spray two 15½" by 10½" jelly-roll pans or large cookie sheets with nonstick cooking spray.
2   Scrub potatoes well, but do not peel. Cut each potato lengthwise in half, then cut lengthwise into ¼-inch-thick slices. Place potatoes in medium bowl and toss with salt and pepper.
3   Divide potato slices between pans and spray potatoes with nonstick cooking spray. Roast potatoes until tender and lightly browned, about 20 minutes, rotating pans between upper and lower racks halfway through.

130
CALORIES

PER SERVING. 4G PROTEIN | 28G CARBOHYDRATE | 1G TOTAL FAT (0G SATURATED) 3G FIBER | 0MG CHOLESTEROL | 305MG SODIUM

GOLDEN CORN MUFFINS

This slightly sweet batter can be baked into muffins or a tender square.

ACTIVE TIME: 10 MINUTES · **TOTAL TIME:** 30 MINUTES

MAKES: 12 MUFFINS

---

1 CUP ALL-PURPOSE FLOUR	1 CUP MILK
¾ CUP CORNMEAL	4 TABLESPOONS BUTTER OR MARGARINE, MELTED
3 TABLESPOONS SUGAR	
1 TABLESPOON BAKING POWDER	1 LARGE EGG
¾ TEASPOON SALT	

1 Preheat oven to 425°F. Grease twelve 2½-inch muffin-pan cups.

2 In medium bowl, with wire whisk, stir flour, cornmeal, sugar, baking powder, and salt. In small bowl, with fork, beat milk, melted butter, and egg until blended. Add egg mixture to flour mixture; stir just until flour is moistened (batter will be lumpy).

3 Fill each muffin cup two-thirds full. Bake until golden and toothpick inserted in center of muffin comes out clean, about 20 minutes. Immediately remove muffins from pans. Serve warm, or cool on wire racks.

145 CALORIES | **PER MUFFIN.** 3G PROTEIN | 19G CARBOHYDRATE | 7G TOTAL FAT (4G SATURATED) 1G FIBER | 40MG CHOLESTEROL | 425MG SODIUM

GOLDEN CORN BREAD

Grease 8-inch square baking pan. Prepare as directed above but use **⅔ cup milk.** Spread batter evenly in prepared pan. Bake until golden and toothpick inserted in center comes out clean, 20 to 25 minutes. Cut corn bread into squares; serve warm. Makes 9 side-dish servings.

175 CALORIES | **PER SERVING.** 3G PROTEIN | 27G CARBOHYDRATE | 7G TOTAL FAT (2G SATURATED) 1G FIBER | 3MG CHOLESTEROL | 385MG SODIUM

LIGHT POTATO SALAD

A healthy variation on the cookout classic, this potato salad utilizes buttermilk and light mayonnaise.

TOTAL TIME: 1 HOUR

MAKES: 6 SIDE-DISH SERVINGS

2 POUNDS SMALL RED POTATOES, SCRUBBED, EACH CUT IN QUARTERS	2 TABLESPOONS LIGHT MAYONNAISE
¾ TEASPOON SALT	1 TABLESPOON DIJON MUSTARD
2 TABLESPOONS DRY WHITE WINE	¼ TEASPOON GROUND BLACK PEPPER
2 TABLESPOONS FRESH LEMON JUICE	½ CUP PACKED FRESH BASIL LEAVES, VERY THINLY SLICED
¼ CUP BUTTERMILK	CHOPPED FRESH CHIVES FOR GARNISH

1 In 5-quart saucepot, place potatoes and enough *cold water* to cover by 2 inches. Cover and heat to boiling on high. Add ½ teaspoon salt. Reduce heat to medium-low; simmer, covered, 8 to 10 minutes or until tender. Drain well and transfer to large bowl.

2 To bowl with potatoes, add wine and 1 tablespoon lemon juice. Toss gently until well mixed. Cool to room temperature.

3 Prepare dressing: In large measuring cup, with wire whisk, stir buttermilk, mayonnaise, mustard, pepper, and remaining ¼ teaspoon salt and 1 tablespoon lemon juice until well blended. (Dressing can be made up to 3 days ahead. Cover and refrigerate.) To bowl with potatoes, add dressing and basil. Toss gently until evenly coated. Garnish with chives.

160 CALORIES

PER SERVING. 4G PROTEIN | 32G CARBOHYDRATE | 2G TOTAL FAT (0G SATURATED) 3G FIBER | 2MG CHOLESTEROL | 135MG SODIUM

BANANA QUICK BREAD

Made with white whole-wheat flour to up the fiber quotient, our sweet, moist banana bread is a delicious quick breakfast, snack, or dessert.

ACTIVE TIME: 15 MINUTES · **TOTAL TIME:** 1 HOUR 15 MINUTES

MAKES: 12 SERVINGS

2 CUPS WHITE WHOLE-WHEAT FLOUR (SEE TIP)

1½ TEASPOONS BAKING POWDER

½ TEASPOON BAKING SODA

½ TEASPOON SALT

¼ TEASPOON GROUND CINNAMON

½ CUP PACKED BROWN SUGAR

2 LARGE EGG WHITES

1 LARGE EGG

4 RIPE BANANAS, MASHED (1½ CUPS)

⅓ CUP BUTTERMILK

3 TABLESPOONS VEGETABLE OIL

1 Preheat oven to 350°F. Lightly coat 9" by 5" loaf pan with nonstick baking spray.

2 In medium bowl, whisk together flour, baking powder and soda, salt, and cinnamon.

3 In large bowl, with mixer on medium-high speed, beat sugar, egg whites, and egg until almost doubled in volume. On medium speed, beat in bananas, buttermilk, and oil until well combined.

4 With rubber spatula, gently fold in flour mixture until just combined.

5 Pour batter into prepared pan, smoothing top. Bake 1 hour or until toothpick inserted in center comes out clean.

6 Let cool in pan on wire rack 10 minutes. Remove from pan and let cool completely on wire rack. Can be stored, tightly wrapped, at room temperature up to 3 days or in freezer up to 1 month.

TIP White whole-wheat flour is milled from an albino variety of wheat. It's as healthy as traditional whole wheat—with the same levels of fiber, nutrients, and minerals—but it has a lighter texture that makes it perfect for baked goods. Gold Medal and King Arthur Flour make it, and there are also health-food-store options to choose from.

170 CALORIES

PER SERVING. 4G PROTEIN | 31G CARBOHYDRATE | 4G TOTAL FAT (1G SATURATED) 4G FIBER | 16MG CHOLESTEROL | 220MG SODIUM ♥ ▤

MASHED POTATOES WITH BROWNED ONIONS

A caramelized onion topping makes mashed potatoes even more irresistible. Who knew that was possible? Consider making extra browned onions—they may be as popular as the potatoes!

ACTIVE TIME: 15 MINUTES · **TOTAL TIME:** 45 MINUTES
MAKES: 6 SIDE-DISH SERVINGS

3 TABLESPOONS BUTTER

1 POUND SPANISH ONIONS, EACH CUT IN HALF, THEN THINLY SLICED

2 TEASPOONS CIDER VINEGAR

3 MEDIUM BAKING POTATOES (8 OUNCES EACH), PEELED, EACH CUT INTO QUARTERS

½ CUP WHOLE MILK, WARMED

¾ TEASPOON SALT

¼ TEASPOON GROUND BLACK PEPPER

1 In 12-inch skillet, melt butter over medium-low heat. Add onions, stirring to coat. Cover and cook 10 minutes or until onions soften, stirring occasionally. Uncover; increase heat to medium and cook 15 minutes longer or until onions are very soft, browned, and reduced to ¾ cup, stirring frequently. Stir in vinegar and set aside.

2 Meanwhile, in 3-quart saucepan, place potatoes and enough *water* to cover; heat to boiling over high heat. Reduce heat to low; cover and simmer 15 to 20 minutes or until potatoes are tender. Reserve ¼ *cup potato cooking water*. Drain potatoes.

3 In saucepan, with masher, mash potatoes until smooth. Gradually add warm milk, mashing potatoes until fluffy. Add some reserved potato cooking water if necessary. Stir in salt and pepper.

4 Spoon mashed potatoes into serving bowl and top with onion mixture. Stir before serving.

175 CALORIES

PER SERVING. 3G PROTEIN | 27G CARBOHYDRATE | 7G TOTAL FAT (2G SATURATED) 3G FIBER | 3MG CHOLESTEROL | 385MG SODIUM

OATMEAL SCONUTS

Sconuts, a riff on two breakfast favorites, are pumped full of oats with a hint of nutmeg. Pop extras into a plastic bag and freeze for up to a month (to warm, microwave for about 20 seconds). Round out breakfast with a cup of berries.

ACTIVE TIME: 10 MINUTES · **TOTAL TIME:** 25 MINUTES
MAKES: 13 SCONUTS

2   CUPS OLD-FASHIONED ROLLED OATS, UNCOOKED

2   CUPS ALL-PURPOSE FLOUR

½   CUP PACKED BROWN SUGAR

2½ TEASPOONS BAKING POWDER

½   TEASPOON BAKING SODA

½   TEASPOON SALT

¼   TEASPOON GROUND NUTMEG

½   CUP BUTTER (1 STICK), CUT INTO PIECES

¾   CUP BUTTERMILK

1   LARGE EGG

CINNAMON SUGAR

1   Heat oven to 425°F.

2   In food processor, combine oats, flour, brown sugar, baking powder, baking soda, salt, and nutmeg; pulse to blend. Add butter; pulse until coarse crumbs form.

3   In cup, beat buttermilk and egg. With processor running, add egg mixture and pulse until a dough forms.

4   Scoop dough by ¼ cups onto ungreased large cookie sheet. Flatten each mound into 2½-inch round. Sprinkle with cinnamon sugar. Bake 15 minutes or until golden on bottoms.

235 **PER SCONUT.** 5G PROTEIN | 34G CARBOHYDRATE | 9G TOTAL FAT (5G SATURATED)
CALORIES 2G FIBER | 37MG CHOLESTEROL | 315MG SODIUM

70
CALORIES
*Honeyed Radishes
and Turnips
(page 130)*

VEGGIES & SIDE SALADS

Whether you choose a slow-baked casserole or a quick skillet dish as your main, you'll want to pair it with an equally yummy veggie side. Our Apple Cider Greens, Creamed Spinach, and Kale Salad make eating your requisite daily green vegetables a pleasure, while inventive sides like Crunchy Carrot Coleslaw, Honeyed Radishes and Turnips, and Carrot and Zucchini Ribbons keep mealtime interesting. Our butternut squash roasted with maple syrup and corn on the cob served with a spicy butter alongside are also not to be missed!

KEY TO ICONS

⏱ 30 minutes or less   ♥ Heart healthy   ⊛ High fiber   ▮ Make ahead   ⌂ Slow cooker

CARROT AND ZUCCHINI RIBBONS

Southwestern seasonings make this quick side salad a great complement to summer's grilled foods.

TOTAL TIME: 20 MINUTES

MAKES: 4 FIRST-COURSE SERVINGS

In large bowl, whisk together **1 tablespoon fresh lime juice, 1 teaspoon vegetable oil, ⅛ teaspoon chipotle chile powder,** and **¼ teaspoon each salt ground black pepper**. Use vegetable peeler to shave **3 peeled carrots** into long ribbons. Stop peeling at core and discard. Shave **1 large zucchini** into ribbons; stop peeling at seeds and discard. Cut all ribbons in half. Add ribbons and **¼ cup fresh cilantro leaves** to dressing; toss until evenly coated.

40 CALORIES

PER SERVING. 1G PROTEIN | 7G CARBOHYDRATE | 1G TOTAL FAT (0G SATURATED)
2G FIBER | 0MG CHOLESTEROL | 183MG SODIUM

LEMONY BEAN DUO

Wax and green beans are tossed in a simple dressing and garnished with lemon and mint. For photo, see opposite.

TOTAL TIME: 35 MINUTES

MAKES: 6 SIDE-DISH SERVINGS

Finely chop **¼ cup fresh mint leaves;** set aside. In large saucepot of boiling water, cook **12 ounces green beans,** trimmed, and **12 ounces wax beans,** trimmed, with **¼ teaspoon salt** for 7 to 8 minutes or until just crisp-tender. Drain well. In large bowl, toss warm beans with **1 tablespoon extra-virgin olive oil, chopped mint, ¼ teaspoon salt,** and **⅛ teaspoon ground black pepper.** Transfer to large shallow serving bowl. Grate peel of one-half lemon directly over beans.

55 CALORIES

PER SERVING. 2G PROTEIN | 8G CARBOHYDRATE | 3G TOTAL FAT (0G SATURATED)
4G FIBER | 0MG CHOLESTEROL | 120MG SODIUM

55
CALORIES
Lemony Bean Duo
(see opposite)

APPLE CIDER GREENS

An excellent side dish for holidays or any day.

ACTIVE TIME: 30 MINUTES · **TOTAL TIME:** 1 HOUR 5 MINUTES
MAKES: 4 CUPS OR 8 SIDE-DISH SERVINGS

Remove and discard stems from **12 ounces mustard greens**. Trim stem
ends from **12 ounces collard greens** and **12 ounces Swiss chard** and
remove stems from leaves; cut stems into 1-inch pieces. Cut all leaves into
2-inch pieces; rinse and drain well. In 5-quart saucepot over high heat,
sauté **2 garlic cloves,** thinly sliced, in **1 tablespoon olive oil** over high heat
30 seconds to 1 minute or until golden, stirring constantly. Add as many
leaves and stems as possible, ⅔ **cup apple cider, 1 tablespoon cider vinegar,** and ¾ **teaspoon salt**, stirring to wilt greens. Add remaining greens in
batches; reduce heat to medium; cover and cook 15 minutes.

Stir in **1 cup red cooking apples**, unpeeled and cut into ¾-inch chunks;
cook, partially covered, 10 minutes longer or until stems are very tender
and most liquid has evaporated, stirring occasionally. With slotted spoon,
transfer to serving bowl.

60
CALORIES

PER SERVING. 2G PROTEIN | 10G CARBOHYDRATE | 2G TOTAL FAT (0G SATURATED)
3G FIBER | 0MG CHOLESTEROL | 310MG SODIUM

CRUNCHY CARROT COLESLAW

A mix of cabbage and carrots gives this slaw its crunch; cider vinegar and a little cayenne delivers a bite.

TOTAL TIME: 10 MINUTES
MAKES: 4 SIDE-DISH SERVINGS

In large bowl, with wire whisk, mix ⅓ **cup fresh orange juice, ¼ cup cider vinegar, 2 tablespoons sugar, 2 tablespoons Dijon mustard, 1 tablespoon vegetable oil, 1 teaspoon salt, ¼ teaspoon dried mint,** and ⅛ **teaspoon cayenne (ground red) pepper** until blended. Add **1 bag (16 ounces) shredded cabbage for coleslaw** and **1 bag (10 ounces) shredded carrots;** toss well. Serve slaw at room temperature, or cover and refrigerate until ready to serve.

65 **CALORIES** **PER SERVING.** 1G PROTEIN | 12G CARBOHYDRATE | 2G TOTAL FAT (0G SATURATED) 2G FIBER | 0MG CHOLESTEROL | 385MG SODIUM

GINGER-JALAPEÑO SLAW

Red and green cabbage costar in this Asian-accented slaw.

TOTAL TIME: 10 MINUTES PLUS CHILLING
MAKES: 8 SIDE-DISH SERVINGS

In large bowl, whisk ⅓ **cup seasoned rice vinegar, 1 tablespoon olive oil, 2 teaspoons grated, peeled fresh ginger, ½ teaspoon salt,** and **2 seeded and minced jalapeño chiles** until blended. Add **1 pound thinly sliced green cabbage (6 cups), 8 ounces thinly sliced red cabbage (3 cups), 3 finely shredded carrots (1½ cups),** and **2 thinly sliced green onions;** toss well to coat with dressing. Cover and refrigerate slaw 1 hour before serving to allow flavors to blend.

65 **CALORIES** **PER SERVING.** 1G PROTEIN | 10G CARBOHYDRATE | 2G TOTAL FAT (0G SATURATED) 2G FIBER | 0MG CHOLESTEROL | 480MG SODIUM

SESAME GINGER SPROUTS

Lively, spicy ginger enhances this Asian-inspired side dish.

ACTIVE TIME: 15 MINUTES · **TOTAL TIME:** 30 MINUTES

MAKES: 2 CUPS OR 4 SIDE-DISH SERVINGS

Trim stems and yellow leaves from **1 container (10 ounces) Brussels sprouts.** Cut each sprout lengthwise into quarters. In cup, stir together **1 tablespoon low-sodium soy sauce, 1 teaspoon grated, peeled fresh ginger, and ½ teaspoon Asian sesame oil.** In nonstick 12-inch skillet, heat **1½ teaspoons olive oil** over medium heat. Add **1 small onion,** cut in half and thinly sliced, and cook 5 minutes or until softened, stirring occasionally. Increase heat to medium-high; add sprouts and **1 tablespoon water;** cover and cook 5 minutes or until sprouts begin to soften and brown, stirring once. Remove cover and cook 5 minutes longer or until sprouts are tender-crisp, stirring frequently. Remove skillet from heat; stir in **soy sauce mixture.**

65 CALORIES

PER SERVING. 3G PROTEIN | 10G CARBOHYDRATE | 3G TOTAL FAT (0G SATURATED) 3G FIBER | 0MG CHOLESTEROL | 165MG SODIUM 🖤 🖤

HONEYED RADISHES AND TURNIPS

A bright addition to any menu. For photo, see page 124.

For photo, see page 124.

ACTIVE TIME: 10 MINUTES · **TOTAL TIME:** 30 MINUTES

MAKES: 8 SIDE-DISH SERVINGS

In 12-inch skillet, melt **1 tablespoon butter** on medium-high. Add **1 small shallot,** finely chopped, and cook 2 minutes or until golden and tender, stirring occasionally. Add **12 ounces radishes,** trimmed and cut in halves or quarters, and **12 ounces small turnips,** trimmed, peeled, and each cut into 8 wedges; stir until well coated. Stir in ⅓ **cup water, 2 teaspoons honey, ¼ teaspoon salt,** and ⅛ **teaspoon ground black pepper.** Heat to boiling. Reduce heat to medium-low; cover and cook 15 minutes. Uncover and cook 7 to 10 minutes longer or until most of liquid has evaporated, stirring often. Remove from heat and stir in **1 tablespoon thinly sliced mint leaves** and **1 tablespoon chopped chives.** Garnish with **sprigs of mint.**

70 CALORIES

PER SERVING. 1G PROTEIN | 10G CARBOHYDRATE | 3G TOTAL FAT (1G SATURATED) 3G FIBER | 0MG CHOLESTEROL | 190MG SODIUM 🖤 🖤

BROCCOLI GRATIN

We've trimmed the fat from a family favorite by using creamy Yukon Gold potatoes as the base of this dish. They make the traditional use of heavy cream and milk unnecessary.

ACTIVE TIME: 10 MINUTES · **TOTAL TIME:** 30 MINUTES
MAKES: 8 SIDE-DISH SERVINGS

1   POUND BROCCOLI FLOWERETS

1   POUND YUKON GOLD POTATOES, PEELED AND CUT INTO 1-INCH CHUNKS

PINCH GROUND NUTMEG

¾   CUP FRESHLY GRATED PARMESAN CHEESE

½   TEASPOON SALT

¼   TEASPOON COARSELY GROUND BLACK PEPPER

1   In 4-quart saucepan, place broccoli, potatoes, and 2 *cups water*. Cover and heat to boiling over high heat. Reduce heat to medium-low; cover and cook until potatoes and broccoli are very tender, 17 to 20 minutes, stirring once halfway through cooking.

2   Meanwhile, preheat broiler and set rack 6 inches from source of heat.

3   Drain vegetables in colander set over large bowl, reserving ¼ *cup cooking water*. Return vegetables to saucepan. With potato masher or slotted spoon, coarsely mash vegetables, adding some reserved vegetable cooking water if mixture seems dry. Stir in nutmeg, ¼ cup Parmesan, salt, and pepper.

4   In broiler-safe shallow 1- to 1½-quart baking dish, spread vegetable mixture; sprinkle with remaining ½ cup Parmesan. Place dish in oven and broil until cheese is browned, 2 to 3 minutes.

TIP The unbaked casserole can be refrigerated up to 1 day. Just bake it 10 minutes longer than directed in the recipe.

95 CALORIES

PER SERVING. 6G PROTEIN | 13G CARBOHYDRATE | 3G TOTAL FAT (2G SATURATED) 2G FIBER | 6MG CHOLESTEROL | 305MG SODIUM ♥ ♥ 🍽

MAPLE SQUASH

In the vegetable department, nothing evokes the fall season like butternut squash. Here we toss it with a mix of maple syrup and spices to give it a hint of heat and smoke flavor, then roast it, which concentrates the vegetable's natural sweetness.

ACTIVE TIME: 5 MINUTES · **TOTAL TIME:** 35 MINUTES
MAKES: 8 SIDE-DISH SERVINGS

Preheat oven to 425°F. Line 15½" by 10½" jelly-roll pan with foil. Place **1 package (2 pounds) peeled and cubed butternut squash** in pan; drizzle with **1 tablespoon olive oil,** sprinkle with **¼ teaspoon salt,** and toss to combine. Roast 15 minutes. Meanwhile, in 1-cup liquid measuring cup, stir ⅓ **cup maple syrup** with **½ teaspoon pumpkin-pie spice** and **pinch cayenne (ground red) pepper**. Toss squash with maple mixture. Continue roasting until fork-tender, 15 to 20 minutes longer. Spoon squash, along with any pan juices, into serving dish.

100
CALORIES
PER SERVING. 1G PROTEIN | 22G CARBOHYDRATE | 2G TOTAL FAT (0G SATURATED) 2G FIBER | 0MG CHOLESTEROL | 80MG SODIUM

CORN ON THE COB WITH SPICY BUTTER

You can easily vary the spices, or try adding fresh herbs to the butter.

TOTAL TIME: 40 MINUTES
MAKES: 6 SIDE-DISH SERVINGS

In medium bowl, mix **¼ cup (½ stick) butter, ¼ teaspoon smoked paprika,** and **pinch cayenne (ground red) pepper** until well blended. Spoon into serving bowl; cover and refrigerate. Heat 5-quart covered saucepot of water to boiling on high. Add **6 small ears corn,** husks and silks removed, and return to boiling. Reduce heat to low; cover and simmer 5 minutes. Drain well. Place on large platter; serve hot with spiced butter alongside.

130
CALORIES
PER SERVING. 2G PROTEIN | 13G CARBOHYDRATE | 9G TOTAL FAT (5G SATURATED) 3G FIBER | 22MG CHOLESTEROL | 95MG SODIUM

CREAMED SPINACH

Even those who swear they hate spinach may be seduced by this mild and creamy dish. For spinach lovers, it's heaven by the spoonful.

ACTIVE TIME: 20 MINUTES · **TOTAL TIME:** 35 MINUTES

MAKES: 6 SIDE-DISH SERVINGS

---

2   TABLESPOONS BUTTER OR MARGARINE

3   LARGE SHALLOTS, FINELY CHOPPED

2   TABLESPOONS ALL-PURPOSE FLOUR

½   CUP MILK

¾   TEASPOON SALT

¼   TEASPOON COARSELY GROUND BLACK PEPPER

⅛   TEASPOON GROUND NUTMEG

1   SMALL PACKAGE (3 OUNCES) CREAM CHEESE, SOFTENED AND CUT INTO PIECES

3   PACKAGES (10 OUNCES EACH) FROZEN CHOPPED SPINACH, THAWED AND SQUEEZED DRY

1   CUP LOOSELY PACKED FRESH PARSLEY LEAVES

¼ CUP SOUR CREAM

1 In 4-quart saucepan, melt butter over medium-low heat. Add shallots and cook, stirring frequently, until tender, about 3 minutes. Add flour and cook, stirring, 1 minute. With wire whisk, gradually whisk in milk; heat to boiling, whisking constantly. Reduce heat and simmer, stirring occasionally with wooden spoon until sauce has thickened and boils, about 2 minutes. Stir in salt, pepper, and nutmeg.

2 Remove from heat; stir in cream cheese until smooth. Stir in spinach, parsley, and sour cream; heat through, stirring frequently (do not boil).

---

180 CALORIES

PER SERVING. 7G PROTEIN | 14G CARBOHYDRATE | 12G TOTAL FAT (7G SATURATED) 5G FIBER | 33MG CHOLESTEROL | 500MG SODIUM

CORN AND AVOCADO SALAD

The piquant citrus punch of lime and cilantro is the perfect pairing for sweet corn, garden-ripe tomatoes, and avocado.

TOTAL TIME: 10 MINUTES

MAKES: 4 SIDE-DISH SERVINGS

2   CUPS FRESH CORN KERNELS OR 1 PACKAGE (10 OUNCES) FROZEN WHOLE-KERNEL CORN, THAWED

1   RIPE MEDIUM TOMATO (6 TO 8 OUNCES), CUT INTO ½-INCH PIECES

2   TABLESPOONS CHOPPED FRESH CILANTRO

2   TABLESPOONS FRESH LIME JUICE

1   TABLESPOON OLIVE OIL

¼   TEASPOON SALT

¼   TEASPOON SUGAR

1   RIPE MEDIUM AVOCADO

LETTUCE LEAVES (OPTIONAL)

In medium bowl, combine corn, tomato, cilantro, lime juice, oil, salt, and sugar. Just before serving, cut avocado in half; remove seed and peel. Cut avocado into ½-inch pieces; toss with corn mixture. Serve on lettuce leaves, if you like.

180 CALORIES

PER SERVING. 3G PROTEIN | 19G CARBOHYDRATE | 9G TOTAL FAT (1G SATURATED) 5G FIBER | 0MG CHOLESTEROL | 196MG SODIUM ● ● ♥

KALE SALAD

This hearty winter salad is not only good for you—it's delicious! For photo, see opposite.

TOTAL TIME: 20 MINUTES

MAKES: 6 FIRST-COURSE SERVINGS

In large bowl, whisk together **2 tablespoons each fresh lemon juice** and **extra-virgin olive oil** and **⅛ teaspoon salt**. Remove and discard stems and ribs from **1 bunch kale**. Very thinly slice leaves; add to bowl with vinaigrette, tossing to coat. Let stand 10 minutes. Add **⅓ cup chopped roasted salted almonds, ¼ cup pitted and sliced jarred green olives,** and **½ cup pitted dates,** cut into slivers. Toss to combine.

180 CALORIES

PER SERVING. 5G PROTEIN | 22G CARBOHYDRATE | 10G TOTAL FAT (1G SATURATED) 4G FIBER | 4MG CHOLESTEROL | 190MG SODIUM ●

180
CALORIES

Kale Salad
(see opposite)

120 CALORIES

Cocoa Brownies
(page 144)

SWEET FINALES

If the first thing you think of when you hear the phrase "comfort food" is dessert, then this chapter is for you. We've provided recipes for lots of old-fashioned sweet treats that are also blissfully low in calories and fat. You can dig into the cookie jar and enjoy one of our Chocolate Chip–Oatmeal Cookies, Pecan Fingers, or Tin Roof Treats without guilt. If you're a certified chocoholic, our skinny Brownie Bites, Cocoa Brownies with mini chocolate chips, or rich and creamy Chocolate Pudding are sure to satisfy. Entertaining? Impress your guests with our Raspberry Soufflé, Strawberry-Rhubarb Crisp, or heavenly Angel Food Cake.

KEY TO ICONS

⬇ 30 minutes or less   ♥ Heart healthy   ✾ High fiber   ▭ Make ahead   ⌂ Slow cooker

RASPBERRY SOUFFLÉ

This impressive fat-free dessert is easier to make than you think; just fold store-bought raspberry fruit spread into beaten egg whites and bake. To get a head start, prepare and refrigerate the soufflé mixture in the soufflé dish up to three hours ahead, then bake it as directed just before serving.

ACTIVE TIME: 20 MINUTES · **TOTAL TIME:** 35 MINUTES

MAKES: 6 SERVINGS

⅔ CUP SEEDLESS RASPBERRY SPREADABLE FRUIT (NO-SUGAR-ADDED JAM)

1 TABLESPOON FRESH LEMON JUICE

4 LARGE EGG WHITES

½ TEASPOON CREAM OF TARTAR

1 TEASPOON VANILLA EXTRACT

2 TABLESPOONS SUGAR

1 Preheat oven to 375°F. In large bowl, with wire whisk, beat raspberry fruit spread with lemon juice; set aside.

2 In small bowl, with mixer on high speed, beat egg whites and cream of tartar until whites begin to mound. Beat in vanilla. Gradually add sugar, beating until sugar dissolves and whites stand in stiff peaks when beaters are lifted.

3 With rubber spatula, fold one-third of whites into raspberry mixture until well blended, then fold in remaining whites. Spoon mixture into 1½-quart soufflé dish; gently spread evenly.

4 Bake 15 to 18 minutes or until soufflé is puffed and lightly browned. Serve immediately.

75 CALORIES

PER SERVING. 3G PROTEIN | 16G CARBOHYDRATE | 0G TOTAL FAT | 1G FIBER 0MG CHOLESTEROL | 35MG SODIUM ♥ 🍽

CHOCOLATE CHIP–OATMEAL COOKIES

Revamped, these gems are still ooey-gooey good—but they're only 80 calories each (with a gram of healthy fiber per cookie). We've also cut out half the fat and cholesterol you'd find in this treat's calorie-laden cousins. Feel free to indulge! Pop extras into a zip-seal plastic bag and freeze up to three months. Reheat 10 seconds in the microwave for a "just-baked" cookie.

ACTIVE TIME: 15 MINUTES · **BAKE TIME:** 12 MINUTES PER BATCH
MAKES: 48 COOKIES

½ CUP PACKED BROWN SUGAR

½ CUP GRANULATED SUGAR

½ CUP TRANS-FAT-FREE VEGETABLE OIL SPREAD (60 TO 70% OIL)

1 LARGE EGG

1 LARGE EGG WHITE

2 TEASPOONS VANILLA EXTRACT

1¼ CUPS ALL-PURPOSE FLOUR

1 TEASPOON BAKING SODA

½ TEASPOON SALT

2½ CUPS QUICK-COOKING OR OLD-FASHIONED OATS, UNCOOKED

1 CUP BITTERSWEET (62% CACAO) OR SEMISWEET CHOCOLATE CHIPS

1 Preheat oven to 350°F.

2 In large bowl, with mixer on medium-low speed, beat brown and granulated sugars and vegetable spread until well blended, occasionally scraping bowl with rubber spatula. Add egg, egg white, and vanilla; beat until smooth. Beat in flour, baking soda, and salt until mixed.

3 With wooden spoon, stir in oats and chocolate chips until well combined.

4 Drop dough by rounded measuring tablespoons, 2 inches apart, on ungreased large cookie sheet. Bake cookies 12 to 13 minutes or until golden. With wide metal spatula, transfer cookies to wire rack to cool.

5 Repeat until all dough is used.

6 Store cooled cookies in tightly sealed containers up to 3 days.

80 CALORIES **PER COOKIE.** 1G PROTEIN | 11G CARBOHYDRATE | 4G TOTAL FAT (1G SATURATED) 1G FIBER | 4MG CHOLESTEROL | 70MG SODIUM ♥

LIME TRIANGLES

Tart filling pairs up with a buttery shortbread crust—what could be better than that?

TOTAL TIME: 1 HOUR 15 MINUTES

MAKES: 48 BARS

¾ CUP (1½ STICKS) BUTTER, CUT UP AND SOFTENED (NO SUBSTITUTIONS)

2¼ CUPS ALL-PURPOSE FLOUR

⅔ CUP PLUS 1 TABLESPOON CONFECTIONERS' SUGAR

5 TO 6 LARGE LIMES

6 LARGE EGGS

1¾ CUPS GRANULATED SUGAR

1 TEASPOON BAKING POWDER

¾ TEASPOON SALT

1 Preheat oven to 350°F. Grease 13" by 9" metal baking pan. Line pan with foil, extending foil over short ends; lightly grease bottom and sides of foil. (If you prefer, use nonstick foil and do not grease foil.)

2 In food processor with knife blade attached, pulse butter, 2 cups flour, and ⅔ cup confectioners' sugar until mixture is moist but crumbly. Dough should hold together when pinched. Transfer mixture to prepared pan; spread evenly. With fingertips, press dough onto bottom of pan. Bake 20 to 25 minutes or until lightly browned.

3 While crust bakes, prepare filling: From limes, grate 1 tablespoon peel and squeeze ⅔ cup juice. In large bowl, with wire whisk, beat eggs. Add lime peel and juice, granulated sugar, baking powder, salt, and remaining ¼ cup flour; whisk until well blended.

4 Whisk filling again and pour onto hot crust. Bake 18 to 22 minutes or until filling is just set and golden. Transfer pan to wire rack. Sift remaining 1 tablespoon confectioners' sugar over hot filling. Cool completely in pan.

5 Using foil, lift pastry out of pan and transfer to cutting board. Carefully pull foil from sides of lime bar. If you like, trim edges. Cut lengthwise into 4 strips, then cut each strip crosswise into 6 pieces. Cut each piece diagonally in half to form triangles. Refrigerate any leftovers.

---

95 CALORIES

PER TRIANGLE. 1G PROTEIN | 14G CARBOHYDRATE | 4G TOTAL FAT (2G SATURATED) 0G FIBER | 35MG CHOLESTEROL | 85MG SODIUM ♥ 🍽

BROWNIE BITES

Espresso powder gives these brownies a nice flavor edge. The cocoa frosting takes them over the top.

ACTIVE TIME: 30 MINUTES · TOTAL TIME: 40 MINUTES
MAKES: ABOUT 28 COOKIES

BROWNIE BITES

- 1 TEASPOON INSTANT ESPRESSO COFFEE POWDER
- 1 TEASPOON HOT WATER
- ½ CUP UNSWEETENED COCOA
- ⅓ CUP ALL-PURPOSE FLOUR
- ⅓ CUP WHOLE-WHEAT FLOUR
- ½ TEASPOON BAKING POWDER
- ¼ TEASPOON SALT
- ⅛ TEASPOON GROUND CINNAMON
- ¾ CUP SUGAR
- 3 TABLESPOONS CANOLA OIL
- 2 TABLESPOONS HONEY
- 1 TEASPOON VANILLA EXTRACT
- 1 LARGE EGG WHITE

FROSTING

- 1 OUNCE UNSWEETENED CHOCOLATE, COARSELY CHOPPED
- 3 TABLESPOONS WATER
- 1 TEASPOON TRANS-FAT-FREE VEGETABLE-OIL SPREAD (60 TO 70% OIL)
- ⅔ CUP CONFECTIONERS' SUGAR
- ½ TEASPOON VANILLA EXTRACT

1 Prepare brownie bites: Preheat oven to 350°F. Grease large cookie sheet. In cup, stir espresso powder into hot water until dissolved. Set aside.

2 In large bowl, combine cocoa, all-purpose and whole-wheat flours, baking powder, salt, and cinnamon. In medium bowl, whisk sugar, oil, honey, vanilla, egg white, and espresso mixture until mixed. With spoon, stir oil mixture into flour mixture, then with hands, press into a dough.

3 With lightly greased hands, shape dough by rolling heaping teaspoons into 1-inch balls; place on prepared cookie sheet, 2 inches apart, and press to flatten slightly. Bake until brownies have cracked slightly, 7 to 8 minutes. Transfer to wire rack to cool. Repeat with remaining dough.

4 Prepare frosting: In microwave-safe small bowl, heat chocolate and water in microwave oven on High 45 seconds; stir until smooth. Stir in vegetable oil spread, then confectioners' sugar and vanilla. Cool frosting slightly. Dip top of each brownie bite in frosting. Set aside to allow frosting to dry. Store in tightly covered container up to 3 days.

---

100 CALORIES

PER COOKIE. 1G PROTEIN | 19G CARBOHYDRATE | 3G TOTAL FAT (0G SATURATED) 0G FIBER | 0MG CHOLESTEROL | 74MG SODIUM

ANGEL FOOD CAKE

Beloved for its clean flavor and light texture, this classic cake has an added attraction—it's low in both calories and fat.

ACTIVE TIME: 30 MINUTES · **TOTAL TIME:** 1 HOUR 5 MINUTES
MAKES: 16 SERVINGS

1 CUP CAKE FLOUR (NOT SELF-RISING)	½ TEASPOON SALT
½ CUP CONFECTIONERS' SUGAR	1¼ CUPS GRANULATED SUGAR
1⅔ CUPS EGG WHITES (FROM 12 TO 14 LARGE EGGS)	2 TEASPOONS VANILLA EXTRACT
	½ TEASPOON ALMOND EXTRACT
1½ TEASPOONS CREAM OF TARTAR	

1 Preheat oven to 375°F. Sift flour and confectioners' sugar through sieve set over small bowl.

2 In large bowl, with mixer on medium speed, beat egg whites, cream of tartar, and salt until foamy. Increase speed to medium-high; beat until soft peaks form when beaters are lifted. Sprinkle in granulated sugar, 2 tablespoons at a time, beating until sugar has dissolved and egg whites stand in stiff, glossy peaks when beaters are lifted. Beat in vanilla and almond extracts.

3 Transfer egg-white mixture to larger bowl. Sift flour mixture, one-third at a time, over beaten egg whites; fold in with rubber spatula just until flour mixture is no longer visible. Do not overmix.

4 Scrape batter into ungreased 9- to 10-inch tube pan; spread evenly. Bake until cake springs back when lightly pressed, 35 to 40 minutes. Invert cake in pan onto larger metal funnel or bottle; cool completely in pan. Run thin knife around cake to loosen from side and center tube of pan. Remove from pan and place on cake plate.

115 CALORIES

PER SERVING. 3G PROTEIN | 25G CARBOHYDRATE | 0G TOTAL FAT | 0G FIBER
0MG CHOLESTEROL | 114MG SODIUM ♥ 🍱

COCOA BROWNIES

Rich cocoa brownies studded with mini chocolate chips figure prominently in our vision of comfort food. We like to cool them completely before serving because they are sometimes too soft to cut when warm. For photo, see page 136.

ACTIVE TIME: 15 MINUTES · **TOTAL TIME:** 35 MINUTES PLUS COOLING
MAKES: 16 BROWNIES

½   CUP ALL-PURPOSE FLOUR

½   CUP UNSWEETENED COCOA

¼   TEASPOON BAKING POWDER

¼   TEASPOON SALT

6   TABLESPOONS BUTTER OR MARGARINE

1   CUP SUGAR

2   LARGE EGGS

2   TEASPOONS VANILLA EXTRACT

⅓   CUP MINI CHOCOLATE CHIPS

1 Preheat oven to 350°F. Grease 8-inch square baking pan. On waxed paper, combine flour, cocoa, baking powder, and salt.

2 In 3-quart saucepan, melt butter over low heat. Remove from heat; with spatula, stir in sugar, then eggs, one at a time; add vanilla and blend well. Stir in flour mixture. Spread batter in prepared pan; sprinkle with chocolate chips.

3 Bake 18 to 20 minutes or until toothpick inserted 2 inches from center comes out almost clean. Cool brownies completely in pan on wire rack, about 2 hours.

4 When completely cool, cut brownies into 4 strips, then cut each strip crosswise into 4 squares. Refrigerate in a tightly covered container up to 1 week.

120 CALORIES

PER BROWNIE. 2G PROTEIN | 17G CARBOHYDRATE | 6G TOTAL FAT (3G SATURATED) 1G FIBER | 39MG CHOLESTEROL | 100MG SODIUM

PECAN FINGERS

This shortbread-style dough is rolled directly onto the cookie sheet, then cut into fingers after baking.

ACTIVE TIME: 25 MINUTES · **TOTAL TIME:** 45 MINUTES
MAKES: 24 BARS

¾ CUP (1½ STICKS) BUTTER OR MARGARINE, SOFTENED

⅓ CUP PACKED DARK BROWN SUGAR

¼ CUP GRANULATED SUGAR

1 TEASPOON VANILLA EXTRACT

¼ TEASPOON SALT

1¾ CUPS ALL-PURPOSE FLOUR

½ CUP PECANS, CHOPPED

1 Preheat oven to 350°F. In large bowl, with mixer on medium speed, beat butter, brown and granulated sugars, vanilla, and salt until creamy, about 2 minutes. At low speed, gradually beat in flour until just evenly moistened. With hand, press dough together to form ball.

2 Divide dough in half. On one side of ungreased large cookie sheet, roll half of dough, covered with waxed paper, lengthwise into 12" by 5" rectangle. On other side of same cookie sheet, repeat with remaining dough, leaving 1½ inches between rectangles. With fork, prick dough at 1-inch intervals. Press tines of fork along long sides of rectangles to form decorative edges. Sprinkle pecans evenly on top; press gently to make nuts adhere.

3 Bake until edges are lightly browned, 20 to 25 minutes. While pastry is still warm, cut each rectangle crosswise into 12 thin bars. Transfer to wire rack to cool. Store in tightly covered container up to 1 week.

120 CALORIES **PER BAR.** 1G PROTEIN | 12G CARBOHYDRATE | 8G TOTAL FAT (4G SATURATED) 0G FIBER | 15MG CHOLESTEROL | 90MG SODIUM

TIN ROOF TREATS

These nostalgic cereal treats celebrate the sweet-salty combination featured in tin roof sundaes, a chocolate sundae topped with salted, red-skinned Spanish peanuts popular in the early twentieth century.

ACTIVE TIME: 20 MINUTES PLUS CHILLING
MAKES: 16 BARS

½ CUP CREAMY PEANUT BUTTER

24 LARGE MARSHMALLOWS

4 CUPS PUFFED RICE CEREAL

⅔ CUP SEMISWEET CHOCOLATE CHIPS

2 TABLESPOONS ROASTED, SALTED SPANISH PEANUTS, CHOPPED

1 Line bottom of 8-inch square baking pan with foil, leaving extra foil on two opposite sides to serve as handles after baking; spray with nonstick cooking spray.

2 In microwave-safe 4-quart bowl, combine peanut butter and marshmallows. Cover bowl with vented plastic wrap and cook in microwave on High 1 minute, until melted. With rubber spatula, quickly stir in puffed rice until evenly coated. With hand, evenly pat puffed rice mixture into prepared baking pan.

3 In microwave-safe cup, heat chocolate in microwave on High 35 to 45 seconds, or until soft; stir until smooth. With offset spatula, spread melted chocolate on top of puffed rice mixture. Sprinkle with peanuts; gently press so nuts adhere to chocolate.

4 Refrigerate until chocolate is set, 30 minutes. Lift foil, with pastry, out of pan; peel foil away from sides. Cut lengthwise into 4 strips, then cut each strip crosswise into 4 pieces. With small metal spatula, separate treats. Store in tightly covered container up to 3 days.

135 CALORIES

PER BAR. 3G PROTEIN | 18G CARBOHYDRATE | 7G TOTAL FAT (2G SATURATED) 1G FIBER | 0MG CHOLESTEROL | 51MG SODIUM ♥ 🍴

STRAWBERRY-RHUBARB CRISP

This sweet-tart confection is just as tasty as Grandma's strawberry-rhubarb pie—but with one-fifth the calories. A whole-grain crumble slashes the fat, while a splash of citrus enhances the sweetness of the berries, making up for almost two cups sugar. Got a spoon? Dig in!

ACTIVE TIME: 15 MINUTES · **TOTAL TIME:** 1 HOUR PLUS COOLING
MAKES: 8 SERVINGS

1 SMALL ORANGE	⅓ CUP OLD-FASHIONED OATS, UNCOOKED
1 POUND STRAWBERRIES, HULLED AND EACH CUT IN HALF	⅓ CUP PACKED DARK BROWN SUGAR
10 OUNCES RHUBARB, TRIMMED AND CUT INTO ½-INCH-THICK SLICES	¼ CUP WHOLE-WHEAT FLOUR
	PINCH SALT
¼ CUP GRANULATED SUGAR	3 TABLESPOONS BUTTER OR MARGARINE, SLIGHTLY SOFTENED
1 TABLESPOON CORNSTARCH	

1 Preheat oven to 375°F. From orange, grate peel and divide between two large bowls; squeeze ¼ cup orange juice into small measuring cup.
2 In one large bowl with peel, combine strawberries, rhubarb, and granulated sugar until well mixed. To measuring cup with juice, add cornstarch; stir until well mixed. Stir juice mixture into fruit mixture until well combined. Pour into 9-inch glass or ceramic pie plate; spread filling in even layer.
3 In other large bowl with peel, combine oats, brown sugar, flour, and salt. With pastry blender or with fingertips, blend in butter until mixture forms coarse crumbs with some pea-size pieces remaining.
4 Sprinkle oat mixture evenly over strawberry mixture. Place pie plate on foil-lined cookie sheet to catch any drips. Bake 45 minutes or until topping is golden brown and fruit filling is hot and bubbling.
5 Cool rhubarb crisp on wire rack until filling is set but still slightly warm, at least 1 hour.

155 CALORIES

PER SERVING. 2G PROTEIN | 27G CARBOHYDRATE | 5G TOTAL FAT (3G SATURATED) 2G FIBER | 12MG CHOLESTEROL | 70MG SODIUM

CHOCOLATE PUDDING

Retro food at its best—and who doesn't love chocolate pudding? This treat has only 2 grams of fat per serving and tastes divine warm or chilled.

ACTIVE TIME: 5 MINUTES · **TOTAL TIME:** 10 MINUTES
MAKES: 4 SERVINGS

⅓ CUP SUGAR

¼ CUP CORNSTARCH

3 TABLESPOONS UNSWEETENED COCOA

PINCH SALT

2 CUPS NONFAT MILK

1 SQUARE (1 OUNCE) SEMISWEET CHOCOLATE, FINELY CHOPPED

1 TEASPOON VANILLA EXTRACT

1 In 2-quart saucepan, with wire whisk, mix sugar, cornstarch, cocoa, and salt until combined. Whisk in milk until blended. Heat mixture to boiling over medium heat, stirring constantly. Add chocolate; cook 1 minute, stirring, until chocolate has melted and pudding thickens slightly. Remove from heat; stir in vanilla.

2 Spoon pudding into custard cups. Serve warm or place plastic wrap directly on surface of pudding and refrigerate to serve cold later.

180 CALORIES **PER SERVING.** 5G PROTEIN | 37G CARBOHYDRATE | 2G TOTAL FAT (0G SATURATED) 1G FIBER | 2MG CHOLESTEROL | 105MG SODIUM 🟢 ♥ 🍴

GENERAL INDEX

Note: Page numbers in **bold** indicate recipe category summaries/overviews.

INDEX OF RECIPES BY ICON

This index makes it easy to search recipes by category, including 30 minutes or less, heart-healthy, high-fiber, make-ahead, and slow-cooker dishes.

🌀 HIGH FIBER

Want to get more fill-you-up fiber into your diet? Incorporate the following high fiber dishes into your regular repertoire. Each of these recipes contains 5 grams or more fiber per serving.

🍱 MAKE AHEAD

For convenience, you can make all (or a portion) of these recipes ahead of time. The individual recipes indicate which steps you can do-ahead or how long you can refrigerate or freeze the completed dish.

🏠 SLOW COOKER

These slow-cooked dishes make it easy to get dinner on the table. Just put all the ingredients in the bowl of your slow cooker in the A.M., and you'll have a delicious, ready-to-serve main dish in the P.M.

PHOTOGRAPHY CREDITS

James Baigrie: 9, 25, 46, 63, 90, 95, 102, 107
Monica Buck: 54, 71
Getty Images: Renee Comet/Food Pix, 15; Stok-Yard Studio, 12 (top)
Brian Hagiwara: 75
iStockPhoto: Paul Johnson, 120; Vikif, 149
Rita Maas: 6, 14, 31
Kate Mathis: 18, 35, 51, 110, 124, 136, 145, 147
Ted Morrison: 13
Con Poulos: 21, 71, 87, 99
David Prince: 28, 39
Alan Richardson: 138
Kate Sears: 43, 114, 117, 127
Stockfood: Keller & Keller Photography, 142; Lew Robertson, 12 (top); Chengyu Zheng, 133
Ann Stratton: 118, 128
Studio D: Philip Friedman, 7, 79, 93
Anna Williams: 11, 36, 59, 67, 82, 135

Front Cover: Kate Sears
Spine: Kate Mathis
Back Cover: David Prince (left), Kate Mathis (right)

METRIC EQUIVALENTS

The recipes that appear in this cookbook use the standard United States method for measuring liquid and dry or solid ingredients (teaspoons, tablespoons, and cups). The information on this chart is provided to help cooks outside the U.S. successfully use these recipes. All equivalents are approximate.

METRIC EQUIVALENTS FOR DIFFERENT TYPES OF INGREDIENTS

A standard cup measure of a dry or solid ingredient will vary in weight depending on the type of ingredient. A standard cup of liquid is the same volume for any type of liquid. Use the following chart when converting standard cup measures to grams (weight) or milliliters (volume).

Standard Cup	Fine Powder (e.g. flour)	Grain (e.g. rice)	Granular (e.g. sugar)	Liquid Solids (e.g. butter)	Liquid (e.g. milk)
1	140 g	150 g	190 g	200 g	240 ml
¾	105 g	113 g	143 g	150 g	180 ml
⅔	93 g	100 g	125 g	133 g	160 ml
½	70 g	75 g	95 g	100 g	120 ml
⅓	47 g	50 g	63 g	67 g	80 ml
¼	35 g	38 g	48 g	50 g	60 ml
⅛	18 g	19 g	24 g	25 g	30 ml

USEFUL EQUIVALENTS FOR LIQUID INGREDIENTS BY VOLUME

¼ tsp	=					1 ml	
½ tsp	=					2 ml	
1 tsp	=					5 ml	
3 tsp	=	1 tbls	=		½ fl oz =	15 ml	
		2 tbls	=	⅛ cup =	1 fl oz =	30 ml	
		4 tbls	=	¼ cup =	2 fl oz =	60 ml	
		5⅓ tbls	=	⅓ cup =	3 fl oz =	80 ml	
		8 tbls	=	½ cup =	4 fl oz =	120 ml	
		10⅔ tbls	=	⅔ cup =	5 fl oz =	160 ml	
		12 tbls	=	¾ cup =	6 fl oz =	180 ml	
		16 tbls	=	1 cup =	8 fl oz =	240 ml	
		1 pt	=	2 cups =	16 fl oz =	480 ml	
		1 qt	=	4 cups =	32 fl oz =	960 ml	
					33 fl oz =	1000 ml	= 1 L

USEFUL EQUIVALENTS FOR DRY INGREDIENTS BY WEIGHT
(To convert ounces to grams, multiply the number of ounces by 30.)

1 oz	=	¹⁄₁₆ lb	=	30 g
2 oz	=	¼ lb	=	120 g
4 oz	=	½ lb	=	240 g
8 oz	=	¾ lb	=	360 g
16 oz	=	1 lb	=	480 g

USEFUL EQUIVALENTS LENGTH
(To convert inches to centimeters, multiply the number of inches by 2.5.)

1 in =		2.5 cm
6 in = ½ ft =		15 cm
12 in = 1 ft =		30 cm
36 in = 3 ft = 1 yd		= 90 cm
40 in =		100 cm = 1 m

USEFUL EQUIVALENTS FOR COOKING/OVEN TEMPERATURES

	Fahrenheit	Celsius	Gas Mark
Freeze Water	32° F	0° C	
Room Temperature	68° F	20° C	
Boil Water	212° F	100° C	
Bake	325° F	160° C	3
	350° F	180° C	4
	375° F	190° C	5
	400° F	200° C	6
	425° F	220° C	7
	450° F	230° C	8
Broil			Grill

THE GOOD HOUSEKEEPING TRIPLE-TEST PROMISE

At *Good Housekeeping*, we want to make sure that every recipe we print works in any oven, with any brand of ingredient, no matter what. That's why, in our test kitchens at the **Good Housekeeping Research Institute**, we go all out: We test each recipe at least three times—and, often, several more times after that.

When a recipe is first developed, one member of our team prepares the dish and we judge it on these criteria: It must be **delicious, family-friendly, healthy,** and **easy to make**.

1 The recipe is then tested several more times to fine-tune the flavor and ease of preparation, always by the same team member, using the same equipment.

2 Next, another team member follows the recipe as written, **varying the brands of ingredients** and **kinds of equipment**. Even the types of stoves we use are changed.

3 A third team member repeats the whole process **using yet another set of equipment** and **alternative ingredients**. By the time the recipes appear in our books, they are guaranteed to work in any kitchen, including yours. **We promise.**